JUSTIN THOMAS

BECOME A PROVIDER

Overcome Tragedy, Become Stronger,
and Serve Others Without Burning Out

ISBN: 978-0-578-33414-1

Book Cover by Max Yenin — https://www.yenin.art
Edited by Sophie B. Thomas
Interior Book Design by Casey L. Jones — http://www.CaseyBelle.com

To Mom.

Without you, Pop does not become the model provider. Without your blessing, this book does not exist. You are a hero, and I get the honor of calling you Mom.

Thank you.

CONTENTS

Foreword   vii

Introduction   ix

1. Personal Development for Others   1
2. Speak Every Word as If It's Your Last   9
3. Reflect to Move Forward   22
4. Make Bold Changes   34
5. Create a Provider Vision   47
6. Overcome Obstacles   56
7. Our Turn to Provide   67
8. The Blessing Habits   78
9. The Protecting Habits   99
10. Turn Your Story Around   119
11. Always Provide   130

Epilogue   139

Acknowledgments   143

Works Cited   147

Appendix 1   151

About the Author   153

FOREWORD

I have had the great fortune to provide operational and financial leadership as a CFO to fast-growth startups and companies with billions in revenue and global operations. With a master's degree in counseling and coaching certification from Duke Medicine, I've also provided clinical services in private practice and at the Carolina Clinic Executive Health Center at UNC to a diverse set of clients.

However, outside of being a husband and father, the most rewarding work I have done is in leading a men's mentoring program. Through one of these mentoring groups, I met Justin and learned his story before this one that you are about to read even existed.

From the beginning of mentoring Justin, I observed his intentionality. During the men's group, we talked about a subject to encourage mentees like Justin to love others well and with purpose. In true Justin fashion, with his "Let's Do This!" attitude, he quickly latched on to this topic.

Justin exudes this quality of intentionality as a husband to Amy, father to Penny and Edie, a business leader, a nationally certified coach, and a leader in his church and community, which now includes his own men's mentoring groups that you will learn more about. He is honoring and paying forward to others the Christian legacy his father, "Pop," sought to instill in him.

It's not easy, and Pop was not perfect. This is why we often hide and neglect our calling. But Pop was real, present, and left it all on the table for Justin, his family, and his community. We now get to benefit from those life lessons captured in this reading.

Justin didn't always have a clear calling with all the infographics and lessons you will see in this book. I witnessed a young man who was deliberate in his commitments and relationships. Over eighteen months, I mentored him and celebrated his children's births and promotions in his career, and supported him through the formidable life challenges that are vulnerably described in the following chapters.

This book is a guide for those who want to lay down a legacy of being there, being known, being loved, and loving others well. It is my great honor to collaborate with Justin in his desire that we all leave a legacy of intentionality that leaves no word unsaid or action regretted.

Blessings on your provider journey!

Tim Oakley MBA, MA, CPA
CFO at Prudent Growth Partners & Principal-Thrivers Integrative Mentoring

INTRODUCTION

This book seeks to answer the question, "How can we not only endure life's tragedies, but become a better version of ourselves through them?"

Imagine you are that person, an enduring leader who has faced demanding obstacles, and come out the other side stronger and wiser. One who makes a positive difference in the world without burning out! Are you interested in achieving this future version of yourself? I certainly am, and I'm honored to partner with you on your journey through this book.

As a National Board Certified Health and Wellness Coach, MBA graduate, and experienced entrepreneur, I'm always eager to grow personally and professionally. I've dedicated my life to coaching others to maximize their well-being and performance in life. When I'm not coaching others or building a business, I'm challenging myself to grow, get off the sideline, and back into the game of life, straddling the role of coach and player.

Like you, my journey includes some tragedy, failures, and lessons learned. I've started successful businesses, been awarded student of the year accolades, and interviewed widely successful authors and entrepreneurs through some of my adventures. However, I've also experienced the immense stress of not having enough cash to make payroll, bombing graduate admission tests (thinking my MBA experience was over before it began), and the humble beginnings of recruiting guests to join my podcast.

This book is about you and your journey of living a more intentional life. On the following pages, you will learn more about my life and my father's story. I have tried my best to share authentically to earn the right to be your seasoned guide. I have shared ways I've messed up and some successes to help serve as case studies to expedite your learning, not to show off. If I missed the mark on this objective, please accept my apologies. I am an eager and imperfect provider guide.

Let's get into it because we have some work to do together to be that leader and provider we have always wanted to become, but for some reason, we have found it elusive to grasp.

I hope we all have had at least one impactful voice in our life that positively changed the trajectory of our story. We don't come alive literally or figuratively without the assistance of others. Whether our parents lovingly brought us into this world or attentive mentors filled in the gaps, we have all been provided for, and we have the opportunity to do the same for others.

Countless books have been dedicated to the themes of self-improvement, leadership, and Christian living—this book dances between all of those genres. And if faith isn't a big deal to you, I feel even more privileged to share with you and say welcome to this provider journey!

My hope and prayer is that this book offers you a collection of timeless principles and truths revealed in new and practical ways to assist your personal and professional development.

I believe that to be the provider, we must first provide for ourselves. We need to live with self-love and care to have the energy to bless and protect others. So don't worry, this is not another book simply telling you to "serve more" or "do more" for others. Those are short-term strategies and tactics. I have gained an appreciation for sustained greatness, not just hacks as a health coach and entrepreneur.

Let's not just be one-time providers; instead, the goal is to be an enduring provider. However, there is an enemy along our path: passiveness.

When we sit on the sideline, we miss the opportunity to become a leader who truly matters, and passiveness wins. When we run away from what's most important in our development, we succumb to the enemy of passiveness. Instead, we must learn how to provide for ourselves and serve others to defeat passiveness.

Professionals predict the weather with qualifications in meteorology and climatology. However, we never know when a tragedy in our personal lives or a global pandemic will occur. The good news is that, through some intentional decisions, we can all overcome life's uncertainties.

A couple of years ago, I flew over to Dublin, Ireland to facilitate a retreat. It was for the non-profit my wife and I co-founded called the CL Thomas Fellowship, which you will learn more about in this book. The retreat was a beautiful scene. Men and women whom I had never met, all desiring to learn how to be a better spouse, parent, and friend were thanking me for the opportunity to engage in this retreat. So how did my personal desire of becoming a better provider spread from an idea I had in North Carolina to this international mix of Filipinos and Europeans in Ireland? This was crazy!

I laughed to myself during the retreat and tried to appreciate the moment the best I could. It has been a long, painful journey, and I am excited to share it with you because I believe it can help anyone become a better leader and leave a positive and lasting legacy.

So, why does this updated and expanded version exist? After mentoring more individuals, testing the original provider habits, and experiencing the first global pandemic in 100 years, there were simply more lessons to share. It's my privilege to offer more transformational story details and provide new practical tools for your benefit.

We all need those positive voices in our lives to make real, meaningful change. I hope this updated book will encourage you to surrender the habits that are holding you back and start developing new ones that will provide for you and others.

Bless & Protect,

Justin Thomas
November 2021

CHAPTER 1

Personal Development for Others

"Justin, what do you spend your money effortlessly on?"

I felt all the other workshop participants adjust in their seats to stare directly at me. My wife, Amy, and I had been enjoying a relaxing couples' weekend retreat together at a nice hotel, but now I was on the hot seat. The meeting facilitator started the session by asking me to open up about my finances.

How we spend our money is a personal question that most of us would rather avoid or smudge the truth. But since my wife was sitting next to me, I had extra accountability and knew what the honest answer was.

"Personal development," I confided to the onlooking group.

Whenever I had a goal and believed a person, diploma, or service could help achieve it, I'd pay without hesitation. I consistently invested in my personal and professional growth through education, certifications, personal coaching, and workshops.

I immediately felt a twinge of embarrassment. After all, the theme of this retreat was generosity! My answer was like trying to mix oil and water. Personal development didn't belong in a discussion about living generously. I started feeling guilty and more uncomfortable about my response. Was I wrong to invest in myself in so many ways?

My wife's loving laugh interrupted my thoughts, and she squeezed my hand to confirm I had passed the test through my accurate answer. I took that as a positive sign of surviving the hot seat moment, and apparently, the facilitator did as well. Satisfied with my response, he moved on, but I was stuck in thought. So I returned to the question, wrestling again with my answer: was it wrong to invest so much in myself?

I thought about my MBA diploma hanging in my office overlooking the volumes of personal help, spiritual growth, and business strategy books that filled the bookshelf. Then I recalled a meeting scheduled for Monday with my new executive coach to help discuss my work as the newly minted CEO of a small tech company.

The desire to improve seemed appropriate before the facilitator's question. Yet, as the retreat continued with stories of incredible acts of kindness and generosity, I struggled to grasp how to invest in myself while serving the greater good of others.

Perhaps you fall on the other end of the spectrum where you find it effortless to spend your money on others but struggle to find the time and money for yourself. Both have their benefits and risks.

So what should we do? I ran through the pros and cons during the weekend retreat.

Becoming the best version of ourselves is an admirable goal in life, where we are constantly learning and growing to maximize our God-given skills. However, what is nobler than laying down one's life and giving without hesitation to the needs around us in this fallen world?

The retreat ended and I left with more questions than answers. However, an unexpected letter and call would eventually clarify my thinking and redefine what it meant to grow and give sustainably; to find a comfortable balance between the slippery seesaw of investing too heavily in personal development and serving others to exhaustion. We can all achieve a healthy, lasting lifestyle of investing in our continued growth for the sake of others, or what I like to refer to as becoming a provider.

The dictionary defines "provide" as *to make preparation to meet a need; to prepare in advance; to supply something for sustenance or support.* (Merriam-Webster)

Through my father's story and personal experimentation, I've learned a simple equation to ground me:

Provider = Bless + Protect

A provider intentionally provides for themselves in a way that allows them to bless and protect others. A provider does the necessary work in their own life to bless and protect others in a sustainable fashion that can leave a lasting and positive legacy. That is the proven provider process. Suppose you can develop the habits and skills to bless and protect others consistently. In that case, you will grow into an influential voice and example.

Personal development is necessary to serve others better. However, when we stop investing in our growth, we stunt our ability to provide for others.

I witnessed what it meant to provide for yourself and others through an unexpected call from my father, "Pop."

———————

The phone vibrated. I looked down and saw it was Pop calling. I asked my wife if it was OK if I took the call. It was Sunday night and we were right in the middle of our bedtime routine with our three-year-old and almost one-year-old daughters.

"Sure, I've got this," my wife confidently responded as she balanced one daughter on her hip and positioned a toothbrush perfectly into the mouth of our other daughter. She knew calls from Pop were always purposeful, which meant they were direct and to the point. I should still be available to help finish up the bedtime routine. I answered the phone and stepped into my home office just in time to hear a surprising proposition.

"Well," Pop said over the phone, "I guess it's time to expose myself."

I paused, waiting for Pop to continue. This direct comment came out of nowhere during what I thought was a routine call. What did he mean by that?

"I'm all ears," I said as I sat down in my office chair, ready to listen, now fully concentrating on his every word. I got comfortable, no longer concerned about making it back quickly for bedtime. However, just as he often did, Pop surprised me with his next step. This call was just an initial step towards a more significant moment.

"Let's schedule time together at the Lodge with your brother, John, so I don't have to repeat myself, and you guys can be there together." It seemed he wanted to get something off of his chest and provide something to his sons, to be known by them.

I had no idea what he meant by "exposing himself," but I now knew it would not happen during this call; instead, it was a moment reserved for the Lodge. You didn't push Pop into anything.

I gripped the phone, feeling frustrated and disappointed that I was not going to hear more now. On the other hand, I was also thrilled about the future opportunity to learn more about Pop. I had never heard anything like this come out of his mouth before. With a combination of excitement and perplexity, I wondered what story Pop had to share. He had never even indicated there was anything to expose. I had just been thrown into a mystery plot, and I was eager to hear more.

Pop, who never wanted to be a burden, continued, "It doesn't have to be soon, just a convenient time that works for everybody. Any time will work just fine."

I quickly jumped into action. "I'll talk with John and we will organize a time that works for everyone." I hung up with Pop and immediately called John.

"So Pop wants to share his story with us."

"Ha, what?" my brother exclaimed.

"That's right, he just called out of the blue and said he wanted us both there, and it's up to us to schedule a weekend."

My brother, John, and I quickly scheduled our trip to hear Pop's story.

EXPOSED

A couple of weeks later, I was sitting in the car with my brother. We were both lost in our thoughts, wondering what in the world to expect.

We had both packed up our wives and kids and driven up for this moment. While our families stayed in town spending time with Mom, John and I soldiered on to meet Pop at the Lodge. We couldn't decide how to prepare for the moment and decided to stop at the local grocery to stock up on essentials. We felt ready for anything after loading up on pre-made grocery sushi rolls, Doritos, and a six-pack of Coors beers. (Disclaimer: These purchases were all made before my health-coaching career . . . but I still enjoy those items in smaller doses these days!)

As I hugged a turn on the tight rural roads heading into Floyd, Virginia, I finally broke the silence and asked John, "What in the world do you think we are going to hear?"

"I have no idea!" John smiled back.

Neither one of us had been able to gather any more intel from Pop since his phone call. But, even with all the uncertainty surrounding the day, we knew we were about to experience a special moment. Here is what I journaled before the trip:

> God, tomorrow is when John and I go to Floyd to hear Pop's story— or as he put it, 'time to expose myself.' I really want this to be a private, intimate moment and ask that you help it to be a powerful, real conversation between the three of us and you. Thank you for organizing this moment and for ordaining it. May your will be done. May I bring an open spirit and presence to the day, ready to hear Pop's story and to love him and respect him. In your name, Amen!

John and I arrived at the Lodge. This was Pop's favorite place in the world. After retiring from the furniture business, he and Mom sold the home I grew up in, bought a place in town, and also built the Lodge to commence their next phase of life together. Nestled away from civilization, it was not only his safe haven, but an intimate location for our families to spend holidays together and have intentional conversations on the porch overlooking the pine forest planted by my grandfather.

After arriving, my brother and I opened up a couple of beers and sat down at the kitchen table ready, but not demanding anything. You don't rush the storyteller. I intentionally did not bring any notebooks or anything to distract from the conversation. I didn't want to "poke the bear." If Pop was in the mood to share, the last thing I wanted to do was to get in the way. I wanted to be in the moment and savor it. I didn't want to invade his privacy by asking him to speak loud enough to be recorded on my phone or distract the conversation by taking notes. I sat down and tried to be fully present.

The moment was finally here.

My brother and I thought we were providing for Pop with our attendance, food, and beverage. Yet Pop was about to give us a case study into how providing for ourselves can ultimately bless and protect others.

"Feel free to ask me any questions. It may help me remember more," Pop began. John and I sat at the kitchen counter, silent as Pop started to share his story. Over the next several hours, Pop shared more weaknesses and failures in his life than I had ever dreamed existed. I was on the edge of my seat in disbelief. Pop lived up to his initial description of "exposing himself." He genuinely wanted to be known and understood by his sons. It was an incredible moment to experience.

For Pop to become a better version of himself, he needed to share his story vulnerably.

Hearing Pop's story allowed me to appreciate how critical it is to take the self-development and personal lessons learned and share it openly with others. Pop wasn't just exposing his story. He was revealing the secret of living a meaningful life. He was showing us how a provider blesses and protects others.

After hearing his story of how he lived only for himself as a young man before committing to providing for others, I was reminded how we are never done growing. Plus, what's the point if we succeed in a way that only benefits ourselves? If Pop had never shared his story of transformation, it would not have inspired my brother and me to make positive changes in our lives.

I was learning how a provider invests in his life first and then uses that to bless and protect others directly. Sometimes the act of providing can simply be extending an invitation to share transformative life stories.

Pop always had something to give us, whether paying for a meal while together or sending a thoughtful letter when we were away. However, now we were seeing the fruit of investing in ourselves and moments to make an enduring difference.

CHAPTER SUMMARY

KEY TAKEAWAYS

- **Redefine "provider"**: A true provider provides for himself so that he can sustainably give to others. Provide beyond just money. The new definition of being a provider is Provider = Bless + Protect. You must bless and protect yourself and others.
- **Expose to provide**: A willingness to be exposed to others is a way of providing.
- **Self-development is a waste unless it provides for others:** Our growth should benefit others so that when we are gone, our impact remains. We strive to become a better version of ourselves daily with a vision for how it will ultimately and practically provide for others.

CHALLENGE

Is your personal development going to benefit others or just yourself? Think about a recent life lesson you have learned and vulnerably share it with someone else.

CHAPTER 2

Speak Every Word as If It's Your Last

A couple of weeks after the retreat with Pop and my brother, I was back at work on a typical Monday morning. I stood at my desk and opened my laptop. The office was silent and empty as I prepared for the day. I was the first to arrive, and the morning light was just beginning to shine on the empty table and chairs that my teammates would soon fill.

I was entering my fourth year as CEO of a small tech company. We were making strides towards our ten-year vision by hiring a talented team, moving into a hip downtown co-working space, and launching an exciting new product to the market. I was doing what they say to do: "planning my work and working my plan." I had even completed a pre-dawn workout to start the week off right. I settled into my standing desk feeling energized and prepared for the week ahead.

I started writing out my to-do list for the day, a daily ritual to help me identify and prioritize my top three goals.

Just then, my phone broke the silence and vibrated.

I sighed; the distractions were already starting. My early morning routine was being threatened and I felt annoyed at this inconvenience. I glanced down at my phone, preparing to swipe away the notification, and then stopped.

It was a message from Pop. The text simply read "CHP." This was code for "call house phone" and meant "I need to talk to you, but you have to call me." Pop didn't have outbound calling from the Lodge; his resolute decision to save a couple of bucks, despite the constant inconvenience. He still used an old-school flip phone so his texts were short and sweet.

I was ready to jump into work, and having a conversation with Pop this early in the morning was not on my to-do list. But then again, Pop had never texted so early in the morning.

I took a deep breath to move past the interruption in my day and called Pop, still thinking about all my responsibilities for the week ahead.

A man answered the landline but it was not Pop's voice.

"This is Raymond. I'm here with your mom."

He paused before delivering the shocking news.

"Your dad *died* this morning."

My stomach dropped to the floor while my feet braced the impact of the news. My mind, numb to what I had just heard, was unable to formulate any response. Finally, I uttered a weak acknowledgment through the phone.

"What?" I couldn't believe it. I had just recently spent the weekend with him and my brother and now . . . he was gone.

Raymond, a close family friend, spoke matter-of-factly. "We've called the funeral home, and your mom wanted me to call you. Would you like to speak to her?"

"Yes," I replied as my mind spun in circles. One-word responses were all I had to offer in this tragic moment.

This was supposed to be a "normal day" that would fade away from memory due to its standard weekly routines. However, March 20, 2017 would turn into a day I can recall most vividly.

"Hi, honey," Mom struggled through tears. She began to fill me in on the details. Pop had had a heart attack early in the morning. Just like that, he was gone. I would learn more of the miraculous story later. He was only sixty-seven.

Mom continued, "Do you want to see Pop's body before the ambulance arrives?"

I shielded my face from view in case anyone walked down the hallway. I gazed out the office window overlooking Main Street, trying to process it all and what I should do. Just seconds ago I was trying to answer the question, "What are the three most important goals of the day?" Now I was contemplating an entirely new paradigm shift. Did I want to see my father's dead body?

Downtown was bustling along, everyone in an angry rush to get to work, single-focused on the plans of the day. I had been just like them mere minutes ago. None of that mattered anymore.

"No, Mom, don't wait on me," I responded. "I'll be there as soon as I can. I'm only three hours away. I love you."

I got off the phone and took a moment. I stood in the center of the empty office just trying to breathe. I was thankful to be alone as I regrouped myself. Like Raymond, I went into a businesslike mindset. Everything had changed. I needed to prepare to leave the office immediately, but not before messaging the team that my father had passed away and I would be on bereavement leave. I sent a separate message to the Executive Team stating I was going on indefinite leave. With that, I packed my bags and exited the office much heavier than I had entered. I made my way to the parking deck and collapsed in the front seat of my car.

I took another moment for myself by sending a group text message to my closest friends. I notified them that Pop had passed and that I was about to begin my journey back home. Like how Mom asked for help in her own way, I asked these men to take care of me. I didn't need to ask for anything in particular. I was confident they would support me in prayer and however else I would need. I started up the car. I exited the empty parking deck towards the highway and started the drive to see Mom.

I then made the most challenging calls I've ever had to make. First, I called my brother and then my wife. Thankfully my brother answered. He probably thought the same thing I did when I received a "CHP" text so early in the day. Something unusual must have prompted my call so out of the ordinary. After quickly asking my brother how he was doing, I told him I had some hard news to share.

This was the first time I'd said it out loud: "Pop passed away." Instead of delivering the news with Raymond's calm delivery, my voice cracked from emotion as I spoke to my brother. In this moment, I realized I was going south on the highway when I needed to be going north.

John was as stunned as I had been just moments earlier. As I turned the car around, my brother asked if he could pray. While I was fumbling to go in the correct direction, his internal compass was pointed where it needed to be at this moment. This spoke volumes to the man and character of my little brother.

He prayed for our family and honored the legacy of Pop. I remember thinking how it was likely the first prayer for our family during this time of loss. My brother finished his prayer and I told him I was headed to see Mom and that I had not yet told my wife or our sister the news yet. He informed me that he, too, would be on his way after he packed up his wife and seven-month-old son.

I then tried calling my wife. No answer and I elected not to leave a message. Instead, I needed to focus on driving the right way as I tried controlling my emotions.

The drive to see Mom was a blur. Sometimes I would hum along to a song and then stop when remembering the news I had just received. My mind was trying to protect me from the harsh reality of the situation to allow my body and mind to drive safely ahead.

One moment I would feel thankful, and the other moment darkness threatened to overtake me. I would fight off this heaviness with memories of being with my brother and Pop just two weeks earlier for that final guys' weekend. Then I would think about my work and worry about how everything was going to get done. There seemed to be a game of ping-pong going back and forth in my memories between positive and negative thoughts. Throughout the drive, a flood of memories of Pop would jump to the surface. Finally, my racing mind was interrupted when my phone rang. It was my wife calling back.

"Hey," I said. "How are you and the girls?"

"We're fine." She sounded busy. Naturally, she had no idea what had transpired. "We just finished their swim lessons and I'm packing them up in the car now."

I could hear my daughters in the background, laughing. Then it hit me. How do I tell my daughters that their beloved Pop is gone?

Visualizing having this conversation with my oldest daughter was heartbreaking. How do you describe the concept of death to a three-year-old? How do you tell her someone that she knew and loved and that she just saw a couple of weeks ago is now gone? How do you handle the sudden loss of the family patriarch who hand-made a rocking horse and bought his granddaughters their first cowgirl hats? I was devastated by the thought that our one-year-old daughter would never know Pop. I needed to snap out of this internal dialogue and deliver the news to my wife.

"Amy, I need you to be strong for the girls." I was now in tears.

I willed the words out the best I could and shared the news. Pop was gone. I informed her that I was on my way up to see Mom and asked if she could pack up the girls and head up whenever she could. She said she would pack up immediately, and I knew she would. Only my wife could handle the tragic news, manage two girls under the age of four, and pack them up for an undetermined length of time—including funeral clothes—on such short notice.

After speaking with my wife, I remember continuing the three-hour drive without making any stops. A couple of calls and texts came in, some offering prayers and condolences, and some were trying to work out critical business needs in my sudden absence.

I was stirred out of my head when a flash glowed on my dashboard. It was the gaslight indicating I was low on fuel. I was only thirty minutes away and there was no way I was stopping. I pressed on, hoping to make it there before running out of fuel—both for the car and emotionally. Just as I was regaining composure, I turned on to the Lodge's gravel road. The possibility of potentially seeing Pop's dead body brought a restless unease over me as I parked the car. I had finally arrived, and my life, let alone my carefully prepared week, would never be the same.

POP'S FINAL WORDS

My heart was racing as I gripped the cold, brass front door handle before stepping into the living room of the Lodge. I had no idea what to expect. Would Pop's lifeless body still be there?

My first image was a man sitting upright on the sofa. My eyes adjusted to the soft indoor lighting, and I noticed the stoic figure was Raymond, our friend who had delivered the news to me just three hours earlier. Then I saw Mom and we embraced in the living room.

"They took his body," Mom sobbed in my arms. I was relieved; I had no desire to see Pop's lifeless body. All I could do was hang on to Mom. I was standing in this exact spot just two weeks earlier with Pop and my brother for our guys' weekend. Now I was back, but this time holding on to my weeping mother.

After a few moments, Mom released her grip and Raymond came over and shook my hand. I thanked him for being there. Sometimes the best gift is simply being present, and I was certainly thankful for his calming demeanor. Finally, we all sat down on the sectional, stunned at the moment.

Once seated, Mom started to share what had happened. I was impressed that she wanted to speak at all. She was visibly shaken, heart-broken, but a tangible feeling of strength exuded from her body language. She had a peaceful tone as she recalled how Pop had died in this very room just hours ago. Unbeknownst to me, I was sitting in the exact spot where he had breathed his last breath while I listened to Mom share the story.

Mom must have intuitively sensed that I desperately wanted to know what happened to Pop. How could he be gone? What had happened? She saved me the effort of asking for details. Regardless of what you believe, his last moments were just incredible and, dare I suggest, prophetic and divine.

She sat with me, teary-eyed, and started to share the events that just changed our reality forever. I was in a state of shock but I tried breathing slowly to help me focus on her words.

"We went out to dinner last night, and it was a fun night out together."

I smiled to myself. I knew exactly what Mom meant. When Pop was in a bad mood, everyone could feel it. He did not hide anything; he was direct and authentic. On the one hand, what you saw was what you got with Pop, and on the other hand, he lived a much richer and more complex life than what many would believe. I had only recently learned this new insight—more to come on that later. However, I did not let myself linger in the past and once again concentrated on Mom's words as she unpacked the story of Pop's final day.

"We were driving in silence back from an enjoyable dinner together in Pop's car and then . . ." Mom paused before starting again. "And then . . . out of nowhere, he said to me, 'Y'know, I'm not going to live forever.'"

"This was so out of the blue, and I made a joke of it, saying, 'Of course you are! You are going to take care of me,'" Mom replied with a laugh.

After a few more moments of silence, they shifted the conversation and reviewed their plans for the following day. They were going to drive into the city for a fun outing of eating and shopping together. Before leaving for the city in the morning, they needed to pick up Mom's car from the mechanics. Mom thought they were all set with their plans, and then Pop surprised her again.

"Let's get the car now," he said.

"Tonight?" Mom asked. It was late. She was full and tired from a delicious meal and evening out together. Plus the shop would be closed.

"Why wait?" he said.

Instead of getting Mom's car the next day, why not get it right now? So, Pop went twenty minutes out of his way to the mechanic and pulled into the dark shop. He knew the car was ready and how the honor system worked. He stepped out and wrote what would be his final check, thus ensuring he did not owe anyone anything. Pop was a man of integrity, honoring all his commitments and obligations until the very end. The keys were waiting for him in the unlocked car, and they drove home separately in the two vehicles back to the Lodge.

Mom continued the story. "After watching a show, we went to bed, expecting to start the next day as normal. And then . . ." There was that pause again. Mom needed a moment before continuing. "And then, around 4:30 a.m., Pop got out of bed." I felt the tension of wanting to stop Mom from reliving the tragic moment that was mere hours removed while also desperately rooting for her to find the strength to continue. Fortunately, she had the stamina to continue sharing. "When he got up, he said, 'It hurts right here.'" Mom re-enacted Pop, pointing to her chest.

Mom described how they moved out of the bedroom and into the living room to rest on the sectional. Pop was calm but kept saying it hurt in the middle of his chest and that his arms were tingling. Finally, Mom asked if they should go to the hospital. Pop shook his head and asked Mom to find the medical diagnosis book in the house.

It was a solemn moment and they both knew it. No diagnostic book was needed.

"I told him, 'Your chest hurts and your arms are tingling—we don't need a book to tell us you're having a heart attack.'" Mom shared how she was mentally preparing to leave for the hospital. She started to gather her items for the trip into the community hospital. Meanwhile, Pop was praying out loud in a calm fashion that helped to soothe Mom's anxiousness. He was reciting Scripture that was near to his heart and written on the inside of his well-worn leather Bible.

After a couple of minutes of praying, Pop paused. "It feels better." He rested on the edge of the sectional and then asked Mom to put wood in the stove to heat the living room.

The room had a chill as the morning sun still had not yet risen. Mom got up off the sofa, walked over to the woodpile by the fireplace, and placed a new log inside the stove.

As she was leaning by the stove, she heard Pop's final words: "You did a good job."

Mom looked up from the stove to see Pop smiling and sitting upright on the sofa with his hands extended to the sky. A moment later, his hands fell and crossed over his eyes. Pop was gone.

"His last words to me," Mom repeated the statement to ensure I was following along as she spoke, "his last words were so special. I took 'good job' to mean *well done* as a wife, mother, and friend. I just lay there next to his body, crying and praying."

Mom then smiled and recalled, "Pop would joke with me early in our marriage about needing a wife to keep the fire going while he was at work. As a city girl growing up in San Francisco, this was not something that came naturally to me."

We both knew Pop had picked the perfect wife to put the final log on the fire.

POP'S FINAL LETTER

A couple of days later, I stirred out of bed feeling restless. I quietly exited the dark guest bedroom not to awaken my wife or two girls who were all soundly sleeping. We were all staying with Mom as we sorted out what needed to be done in the wake of Pop's death. In the pre-dawn hours of the morning, I tiptoed down the hall towards the kitchen, trying to ensure Mom would also not be disturbed. As I settled down at the kitchen table, I exhaled, trying to breathe some life into my weary body. Things had gotten busy after the moment with Mom at the Lodge the day of Pop's passing. From meetings with accountants, lawyers, financial advisors, and insurance agents, my hard outer shell was starting to crack from the beating waves of activity.

Mom, my siblings, and I had managed to meet together to discuss how we would honor Pop. We all agreed to host a public reception similar to an Irish wake to pay tribute to his life. I told my family I wanted to deliver a toast in Pop's honor. I had no idea what I wanted to say when I volunteered. However, I had a clear vision of standing in front of a crowd, welcoming them and sharing some remarks. Without realizing it at the time, I was moving away from passiveness, asking to take on more and being proactive when seeing a need versus avoiding it.

Finally, alone in the predawn darkness of Mom's kitchen, it was time to think and reflect on this crucial task at hand. Perhaps my most critical public remarks I would make outside of my wedding vows. In two days, I would speak on behalf of my family and deliver Pop's eulogy. How could I use this opportunity wisely? I hoped I would find some inspiration for this task at hand to honor Pop appropriately.

It was time to open the letter.

Two years earlier, I had received an unexpected envelope in the mail with Pop's instantly recognizable handwriting on it. I opened it up only to discover another, smaller envelope. It was sealed with simple instructions: "Put in a safety deposit box, open upon my death." This was classic Pop—no forewarning and no elaborate instructions. After receiving the letter, I had called him up and asked if there was anything I should know about this mysterious note. Pop simply responded to do what it said, and that was that. Again, you didn't argue with Pop. I put it in my safety deposit box where it had remained.

My wife had retrieved the letter after I called with the news of Pop's death. This was an impressive feat considering she had to organize someone else to watch our kids while she ran out to the bank and carefully packed it up along with everything we needed for the week ahead. With all the activities and immediate demands of the moment, I had put this letter on the back burner. Now was the moment to open it and unveil its contents finally.

I searched for the letter, and there it was, tucked away where Amy had packed it. It was addressed to me and I paused, staring at my name. The letter was addressed to me, designed for this moment.

As my eyes started to well up from the sight of Pop's handwriting, I slid my finger under the envelope flap and started to feel the same curiosity and excitement when Pop had confided that he was ready to expose his story. Would this letter bring to light other details of his past?

I pulled out a single sheet of paper and unfurled the crisp letter to finally read this message from the grave:

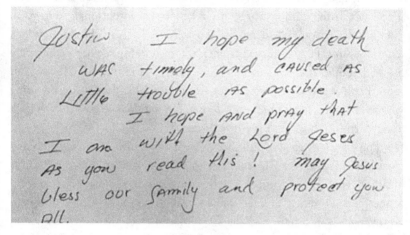

"Justin, I hope my death was timely and caused as little trouble as possible. I hope and pray that I am with the Lord Jesus as you read this! May Jesus bless our family and protect you all. -Love, Pop."

And that was not all. There was a drawing under his signature where I could find cash at the house to help pay for funeral expenses. Classic Pop! He had left me with words of inspiration and a treasure map! I was holding a precious gift in my hands. But, beyond the financial gift, I had been given a more precious asset, a short benediction to carry on in life. It was direct and to the point—which was how Pop always communicated.

This letter served as the inspiration for creating the Provider = Bless + Protect equation.

What would you write to your family at the end of your life? What would you want your final words to be?

The guy who wrote most of the New Testament, Paul, had to say good-bye to some friends, and he chose to share these words of wisdom from Jesus in Acts 20:35b: "and remember the words of the Lord Jesus, how he himself said, 'It is more blessed to give than to receive.'" (English Standard Version)

Both Paul and Pop preached generosity through their final words. Pop's last letter demonstrated his take-charge, intentional strategy in life. He didn't want his death to be a burden. Even in the first few raw days of losing Pop, I was experiencing the soothing feeling of knowing he had thoughtfully planned and prepared his family for life without him. He had a will and left a debt-free estate. This thoughtful planning was even more incredible considering Pop worked in the low-margin retail furniture business his entire career.

Pop had indeed accomplished his wish to cause "as little trouble as possible." He was showing me how to think of others even through his death. I would have probably written a how-to list for my firstborn, something to make me feel smart and important—and that's even assuming I would have had the wisdom and foresight to write a letter! Here was what stood out to me about Pop in the letter:

1. the foresight and intentionality to write a letter prepared for me, and
2. the focus on our family and not on himself.

As I reread the short letter and studied the drawing, I smiled at the thought of Pop with Jesus. It became real to me right then that he was in Heaven. *In Heaven!* This place I supposedly believed in as a Christian but had never really pictured anyone really enjoying. I rested in that vision for a moment and made some tea as a warm glow started to peer over the Virginia mountains.

This letter inspired the theme of my toast. While the beginning and middle of Pop's letter touched me, the closing line became my new rally cry in life. *"May Jesus bless our family and protect us all."* I couldn't just follow the steps in my own strength. I needed Jesus to bless and protect me through this first week of Pop's passing and my upcoming toast.

I started writing my toast about Pop with a new energetic focus. As the sun turned from orange to a yellow hue, I folded back the letter to keep safe. I knew exactly what I would say for my final remarks about Pop. I could only hope and pray they would have a similar weight and impact as Paul and Pop showed me through their final words on the importance of generosity and caring for others. I wanted my toast to be a gift to those in attendance.

Once again, I was reminded of the power of final words. Whether reading his letter to me or hearing Pop's last words of encouragement to Mom, there was a consistent theme of providing for others. I reflected how even in death, Pop was giving to us. I was starting to appreciate how each moment is divine; we just don't see them that way unless we commit to being fully present.

CHAPTER SUMMARY

KEY TAKEAWAYS

- **Assume the moment is divine**: Since we don't know when a moment will be our last, it is not only in our best interest, but that of others, if we treat each moment as divine.
- **Don't wait**: We can all change our default mindset from passiveness to action, whether it is picking up the car from the mechanics or paying our final bills.
- **Believe your words have meaning**: Let's not miss those life-changing moments out of fear. Share your words wisely and bravely. This provides for you and others.

CHALLENGE

What final words can you write or express now? Whether it is a letter to have someone open when you pass or telling a loved one something today, take action to communicate a "final word" today.

CHAPTER 3

Reflect to Move Forward

A n amazing transformation occurred in my life from the time I received that final "CHP" text. I've experienced a new sense of calling and purpose in my life. On the surface, this makes no sense. The father I loved and respected is gone forever, and I dare to claim I am enjoying life more? This all sounds downright heartless. However, my heart had to break to discover this truth, and I hope you can learn the same lessons without a tragic loss.

The secret? To provide for yourself so you can provide for others in beautiful new ways. We become a better version of ourselves when we decide to say goodbye to passiveness forever.

Pop's passing allowed me to reflect on his life so that I could determine how best to carry on his legacy. Adopting a provider mindset has been the vehicle for honoring Pop, and changing my life for the better. I wholeheartedly believe it can do the same for you. A provider who matters receives their provision from God and then provides for others. This allows us all to ensure we do not burn out; rather, we have the strength to provide for others. My father's passing and the subsequent decisions, traumatic experiences, and career events showed me the power of becoming a provider. Adopt a provider lifestyle before you are faced with a crisis like the sudden passing of a parent, and you will be able to act with wisdom while avoiding burnout.

The days following Pop's death convinced me of the incredible gift of being the provider, especially when I was thrown into new and uncharted territory.

I was about to experience the power of reflection. And contrary to common belief, reflection is not a static state. Instead, powerful reflection is an active process involving thinking, reading, crying, and even preparing a speech.

PREPARING FINAL REMARKS

It was time to deliver my final toast to Pop. The date was Friday, March 24, 2017, four days since his passing. It's another one of those days that has secured a spot on the long-term memory reel, especially since it was also my youngest daughter's first birthday.

I wanted to honor Pop's life with authentic and meaningful words, not empty metaphors or forced expressions to soothe the pain of loss. I wasn't trying to elicit cheap, shallow laughs. Instead, I wanted to honor the man through my prepared remarks. Pop had demonstrated a level of preparedness, even before sudden death, and I wanted to manifest that character trait in my toast.

I needed to reflect on his life to move forward with my own provider journey.

Although it took me hours to write, the end product was just a single page. I challenged myself to pick one character trait to highlight. Being clear with a simple yet powerful theme is one of life's greatest communication challenges. Whether writing a one-page toast or a full manuscript, the struggle is real. Yet, the desire to ensure lessons are not lost motivates me to return to this great battle of achieving clarity. For the toast, my goal was to leave everyone with a straightforward message and image of Pop. He was the model provider. I would honor Pop, the provider, through my prepared remarks.

I was in an unfamiliar role of speaking at a funeral/wake for the first time. I had no idea what it would feel like or if I could even get through it. To help strengthen my resolve, I carried Pop's Bible with me and wore his old leather vest as I walked up the stairs to enter the reception area.

A slideshow of classic Pop pictures played while we all mingled, making small talk. Everyone admired Pop's drawings and woodworking pieces that we had put on display for people to appreciate his many artistic talents. In addition, we had strategically placed empty note-books with pens around the room and encouraged the guests to take a moment to write down their favorite memory or story about Pop.

It was nice to see so many people from different eras of Pop's life. Everyone was gracious, and yet still struggling with the shock that he was really gone. After an hour or so, I told everyone to grab a drink from the bar for a toast.

A few minutes later, I stepped back onto the stage. Rather than a traditional pulpit, I was standing in an erected DJ booth area to give the presentation of my life: a toast to my father's legacy. True, it was a nontraditional setting, yet it was just right for who Pop was. It was the type of funeral he would have wanted to attend. Equipped with pool tables in a casual setting and a bar to grab a cold drink to keep the stories flowing.

When I took to the stage, the bar activity stopped and all eyes were on me. No more chitchat or nervous energy could be heard, just felt. For the first time, I felt the weight of being on stage.

I tried to lean into the moment and be fully present. I looked out at the hundred or so people gathered before me and caught my brother's eye. Like me, he knew Pop's full story and would resonate with these remarks. I was now in the zone. I looked down at my one-page toast. After experiencing so many words of wisdom from Pop, it was my turn to share some final remarks. This gathering couldn't properly end without a toast to Pop. I was confident in the words I was about to share. Yet, I was unprepared for the emotions of the moment.

I welcomed the audience on behalf of Mom, my sister, my brother, and our entire family. Then I started to share the following prepared remarks.

THE TOAST

"Thank you for joining us today for this memorial. It is my honor to share some brief remarks about my father, Calvin Thomas. I want to focus our time together on one specific trait and role that he excelled at in life.

That word and role is *provider.*

What did he provide?

On the surface, he provided sixty-seven years of memories from his time here. On the surface, he provided for his wife for thirty-four years. On the surface, he provided financially for his family by running the furniture store for thirty-plus years.

But what Pop really loved was simply providing for his family and those in need."

I stopped to gather myself. My voice cracked as I was surprised my emotions were welling up. I shouldn't have been taken this off guard. After all, this is what being fully present is all about—feeling and acknowledging the emotions. But for some reason, I did not expect to be gasping for air. I needed to reach deeper than I had ever done before to gain composure and share what I so desperately wanted to articulate to the waiting crowd. I breathed in and out to regain my strength and was able to continue.

"Here are just a few of the things Pop did in the last year alone to provide:

He provided a home for my sister and her family, laboring in it with his own two hands, customizing it for the unique needs of his special-needs grandson. This project showed off his wide-ranging craftsman skills, and more importantly, his fatherly love for my sister.

Three weeks ago, he invited my brother and me to meet at his house to hear his life story. During this time, he encouraged us to ask any questions we wanted to. I will forever be grateful for that day and what we shared together.

Just last week, he picked up a hitchhiker in Floyd whom he remembered delivering furniture to during his career. After dropping him off at his house, Pop gave the passenger his nice, warm wool gloves from the car and some money.

And lastly, and even more recently, the night before his death, Pop provided a final meal out for my Mom. And just to put the final exclamation mark on his legacy as provider, on their way back from dinner, instead of waiting until the next day, Pop picked up Mom's car from the mechanics on Sunday night before breathing his last breath by her side Monday morning.

Pop never waited until the next day. He always provided today.

Please join me in a toast. To Pop; the provider who modeled his life after the ultimate Provider, Jesus Christ. Today we celebrate the fact that he is being provided for in Heaven.

To Pop!"

I lifted my drink in the air as everyone shouted, "To Pop!" I had teared up during my remarks but somehow managed to hold it together and deliver the message to completion.

I staggered off the stage and was greeted by my high school speech and drama teacher, a close family friend, who told me it was "perfect in every way." I appreciated those words. I had tried speaking from the heart.

With adrenaline still flowing, I saw my sister, and we embraced. My sister and I were not close at the time; however, we immediately brushed all that baggage aside. As I held on to her, my eyes welled. After hugging my sister, I went to the bathroom for a moment alone.

I used to think it was fun being on stage. Now I am starting to appreciate the burden of leadership.

Shortly after delivering the toast, I returned home to North Carolina with my family.

I hadn't fully realized the harsh new reality of life without a father. The recent busyness distracted me from facing this new reality. I had put on a mask just to get things done. I was even mistaken for the family lawyer at the bank based on my demeanor, questions, and businesslike attitude. We often dress up our brokenness to appear put together, and we pretend that we can wear the disguise forever. But, eventually, the cracks show, even when you carry a leather briefcase to meetings and look like a lawyer!

I could not wear the mask forever. Fortunately, I had amazing people in my life who helped to remove it gently.

First, Mom gave me a book on grieving, called *Winter Grief, Summer Grace* by James Miller. This read was an unexpected gift. I should have been the one providing for her! Instead, she knew I needed support through my own grieving process based on the accurate intuition of a caring mother. It proved to be the first step in loosening my mask. I would have never bought this book independently, yet I was comforted by its mere presence on my nightstand. The gift not only served as a reminder of Mom's love and provision in my life, but it also provided a framework for how to grieve and pause to appreciate the loss before trying to get the next task done by comparing grief to the natural flow of the calendar year.

This book stated that grief is like the seasons; it's natural and necessary, even if we are not ready for it. Winter comes regardless if we are prepared for the chill. In addition, there is no "right" way to grieve, similar to how there is no one way to experience spring, summer, fall, or winter. We all confront the seasons uniquely.

Fortunately, winter is not forever and we are called to honor the current season. But, as much as we may want to, we simply can't skip the natural or emotional seasons of life. The book and framework of grieving freed me to appreciate how my current and difficult survival seasons could lead to rebirth, just as the spring flowers come out after the winter months, ready to bloom.

Second, my friend Brad encouraged me to start journaling to reflect on the events that had just transpired. I told him the incredible story of Pop's final actions and words; he kindly, yet forcefully, told me to write it all down. I'm so grateful he prompted me to make time for this journaling exercise. Not only did it help me in writing this book with accuracy, but journaling allowed me to also reflect on the divine nature of Pop's passing and all the lessons I was being exposed to and learning in real-time.

The writing proved to be therapeutic. I reflected on all the details and moments after receiving the "CHP" text message from Pop's phone. The volume of pages felt more like a full memoir, yet the content only spanned a period of twelve hours. I then outlined all the events the week of Pop's passing and was struck by how much I had done and how little I had rested.

BREAKDOWN

We all need a good cry every now and then. And my mask was finally removed during a coffee meeting with my pastor. Pastor Reggie isn't just a religious figure in my life, he is a friend. We met fifteen years ago during a pickup basketball game when he was a campus minister and I was a recent college graduate trying to start my career in a new town.

Pastor Reggie was not fooled by my claims that I was "fine." We had spoken a couple of times on the phone after Pop's passing, and this was our first in-person meeting since I had returned home. It started similar to our previous conversations, but something broke inside me when he asked a simple yet direct question.

Reggie looked at me with care as we settled into our chairs outside at a popular cafe. "How are you and the family doing?"

"We are good. It's been amazing to see how God has held us all together during this time." I started to recount the major recent events in a methodical fashion, and then something unexpected happened. I heard how casual my tone was. In a sense, I heard myself for the first time and recognized I was back in the "family lawyer" mode. I broke down.

Tears started to flow uncontrollably. Snot coming out, the whole nine yards. I had a single napkin to try to control it all, but it was no match for the sheer volume of tears and mucus streaming down my face. Finally, the dam had broken loose and I could feel the other customers staring at me. I felt like I was making a scene, but it didn't matter. I could wear the mask no longer. Pastor Reggie gave me the space and time I needed before continuing. Honestly, I'm surprised he didn't run to get more napkins so that he didn't have to witness my blubbering mess! Through it all, he was showing me how to be there for a friend in need. I could feel the support; Reggie didn't need to say anything.

I eventually managed to squeak out a more honest response. "It's been tough, Reggie."

I regained my composure when I shared how I was inspired by Pop's legacy of being a provider. He listened intently and then suggested I explore Psalm 23. This surprised me. I associated this famous passage with funerals and death, not providing. I had been given a laminated copy of Psalm 23 from the funeral home as a gift just to confirm how this passage serves as the boilerplate text for all things relating to funerals.

Again, Pastor Reggie encouraged me to read Psalm 23, but this time, through the lens of being a provider rather than a funeral services client. I took his words to heart.

After I met with Pastor Reggie, I returned home and reread Psalm 23, now with a genuine curiosity about how this related to being a provider. The passage reads:

> *The Lord is my shepherd;*
> *I shall not want.*
> *He makes me to lie down in green pastures;*
> *He leads me beside the still waters.*

He restores my soul;
He leads me in the paths of righteousness
For His name's sake.

Yea, though I walk through the valley of the shadow of
*   death,*
I will fear no evil;
For You are with me;
Your rod and Your staff, they comfort me.

You prepare a table before me in the presence of my
*   enemies;*
You anoint my head with oil;
My cup runs over.

Surely goodness and mercy shall follow me
All the days of my life;
And I will dwell in the house of the Lord
Forever. (New King James Version)

I was still grasping to connect this chapter with being a provider. To dive deeper into this well-known chapter, I opened up the *Wycliffe Bible Commentary* and my perspective began to expand when I read the following (emphasis mine):

As a **song of trust**, this psalm has no peer. It is impossible to estimate its effect upon man through the centuries. Grief, sadness, and doubt have been driven away by this strong affirmation of faith. Peace, contentment, and trust have been the **blessings** upon those who have come to share the psalmist's sublime confidence. While the language is simple and the meaning clear, no one has been able to exhaust the message of the poem or improve upon its quiet beauty. (Pfeiffer)

For the first time, I realized how this Scripture beautifully describes blessing and protecting. The "song of trust" implies *protection*. The *blessings* described in Psalm 23 are confidently promised.

Jesus even called himself the Good Shepherd in John 10:11—"I am the good shepherd. The good shepherd lays down his life for the sheep" (English Standard Version). I was now starting to appreciate how Psalm 23 positioned Jesus as our model provider, one who blesses his sheep by selflessly giving of himself to earn the trust of his sheep. Since we are called to imitate Jesus (see 1 Corinthians 11:1, 1 Peter 2:21), we too are called to become the shepherd, the provider.

I continued to explore Psalm 23 through the lens of being a provider, specifically how my father described it as blessing and protecting others.

PROTECTING: PSALM 23:1-4

The first part of this passage shows God as a faithful shepherd. The "epitome of tender care and continuing watchfulness. The sheep instinctively trust the shepherd to provide for them." What a beautiful description and visual of being a provider. You can't protect someone until they trust you. We need to demonstrate a commitment to watching over others like the shepherd watches over his sheep. Someone strong enough to protect, yet tender enough for the "flock" to trust his guidance. Or, as the Wycliffe Commentary describes, "He leads into rest and reviving, into the struggles of life and through the dangerous places. The shepherd thus provides for the needs of life and protects from the fear of danger."

BLESSING: PSALM 23:5-6

The chapter highlights a gracious host extending hospitality to guests with food, oil, and a grand party. The verses promise the guests will be filled with God's blessings. However, it is essential to recognize that the real gift is God himself.

Now I had both Pop's letter highlighting the concept of Jesus blessing and protecting our family, and Psalm 23 describing these same characteristics with beautiful imagery. I had goosebumps. The equation *Provider = Bless + Protect* was etched in my mind as truth. It was no longer just inspiring words for my toast, it was described in Scripture. I felt I had stumbled upon a sacred secret to living a fulfilling life.

I started to read Scripture and pray each morning after returning home from Pop's funeral. Mom gave me Pop's old Bible and I decided to start reading.

As I opened Pop's Bible, I noticed his daily prayer was written on the inside cover. Pop recited this prayer every morning. Mom would hear him say it in the shower or in the kitchen when he was preparing breakfast. He would always start his day out with this custom prayer he had written based on verses that stood out to him from Scripture.

I was stunned—another divine moment. Here was Psalm 23 highlighted for me in Pop's prayer. I could see the specific verses that spoke to Pop, including Psalm 23:4 as he prayed, "I fear no evil for thou art with me, your word and your spirit they comfort me." I loved the rawness of his full prayer handwritten based on his favorite verses. All of its misspellings and imperfections made it more genuine to me. I was beginning to appreciate how much the psalms inspired Pop and why he included them in his daily prayer. It had helped shape a selfish man into a shepherd, the provider I knew and respected. Prayer was an essential element of his personal development and ongoing commitment to becoming a provider.

Pop depended on God's covering to provide moment by moment. This habit of praying a portion of Psalm 23 over his life reminded me of the power of every day disciplined reflection.

——————————— CHAPTER SUMMARY ———————————

KEY TAKEAWAYS

- **Reflection is active, not passive**: To process grief or a transition, the power of reflection, journaling, prayer, and intentional conversations can maximize the lessons and growth.
- **Grief is like the seasons**: Appreciate each season for what it has to offer and realize that everyone can experience them in a unique fashion.
- **Fresh eyes can open up Scripture in new ways**: Whether it is Psalm 23 or another Scripture, we can continue to learn timeless truths if we are willing to have fresh eyes.

CHALLENGE

What are you grieving in life? It could be a lost parent like I experienced or a setback at work or with a relationship. Reserve real, meaningful time to reflect on this loss. Then, capture the good from the grief by practicing active reflection as described in this chapter.

─────── CHAPTER 4 ───────

Make Bold Changes

"I don't mean to take over this meeting, but I'm about to do just that." I paused as I looked at my business partners. "I'm resigning as CEO."

After holding it in as long as I could for the last couple of months since returning from bereavement leave, I was finally taking action. I had played out this exact conversation in my head several times and was now experiencing the moment. This was it. I was leaving.

How did I get to this place of making a bold change? All the reflection had led to inspiration, and I knew it was time for a change.

It all started with a phone call from a friend, some sketches on a markerboard, and a surprising word in the shower.

───────

THE CALL

"Do you think your dad thought of himself as a generous person?"

Silence fell over our phone conversation as I gathered my thoughts. Matt didn't wait for my response. My friend Matt confidently answered his own question: "Because I know I could have asked him for anything, and he would have given it to me."

I smiled, thinking back to my toast and sharing the story of Pop giving the hitchhiker his nice wool gloves and cash after dropping him off home. Of course, Pop was an extremely generous person.

That conversation motivated me to dive deeper into Pop's life habits and characteristics that made him a model provider. I was just starting to capture what it meant to be a modern-day shepherd figure . . . without the sheep.

THE MARKERBOARD MOMENT

After my phone call with Matt, I stepped into my daughters' playroom and sat down in front of their whiteboard. I wanted to tease out this thought and explore the habits and characteristics that define a provider. The whiteboard was set in a wooden easel that was handmade by Pop for my daughters—another ever-present example of his generosity. Reading the "Love Pop" inscription on the inside of the frame, I opened a blue marker to capture my thoughts.

I was searching for a roadmap with practical habits that I could implement in order to carry on Pop's legacy as a provider. I had been blessed and protected by Pop and I wanted to do the same for others.

Pop would have enjoyed how Dr. Jordan Peterson describes why we should reflect and think. "When people think, they simulate the world, and plan how to act in it. If they do a good job of simulating, they can figure what stupid things they shouldn't do." (Peterson 240)

I can't think of a better way of honoring Pop than by taking time to figure out what stupid things not to do—that would certainly make him proud. I also wanted to know the specific habits and traits to actually invest in. So I scribbled more notes on the easel to clarify the most important habits of providers.

THE SURPRISING WORD

After reflecting on Pop's life and sketching out some of the characteristic traits that I wanted to develop, I was struck by another unique word.

As I was considering where to start with this provider experiment, I was nudged by God again. It gets even more strange. The idea came in the shower. As if out of a movie, the word *fellowship* rushed into my consciousness in a sudden way that I could not ignore.

That's a weird word, right? Especially since I was thinking of trying to become a provider. What does "fellowship" have to do with that? I had never received a fellowship or even used that word in my vocabulary. It wasn't related to anything I was doing in work or life. However, the weight of the word stayed with me. I had no doubt that this word came from God. Given all the divine encounters and stories surrounding Pop's life and death, I could not ignore this moment or this word.

I felt as if I was Santiago in *The Alchemist*. In this tale, a shepherd boy is led by omens and moments of inspiration to help fulfill his difficult yet deeply rewarding personal legend. Just like Santiago, I felt like a higher power was directing me, and even though I had my doubts, I, too felt as if I was taking meaningful steps towards my version of a personal legend.

Perhaps God could speak into my life the way I had seen in Pop's life and death. I said a quick prayer, "What does this word mean? Why have you given me this word, God?"

Over the next few days, the word "fellowship" turned into taking my provider journey and extending it to a group, a special fellowship in honor of Pop. Rather than exploring how to climb the provider mountain like a John Wayne figure going at it alone, I sensed a different path being laid out before me in becoming a provider. It would be the same mountain to climb, but I would be journeying with others. I started to get more consumed and committed to this fellowship idea. I would name the group after Pop—the CL Thomas Fellowship.

I have personally benefited from a variety of people and groups in my life. These role models have come in many different forms ranging from my professors and teachers, hired executive and sales coaches, formal and informal mentors, family, friends, and everyone in between. I could not bear the thought of letting these incredible relationships go to waste and only benefit my own personal development. I wanted to take everything and everyone who had provided for me and give that as a gift through a fellowship experience.

I shared the idea of starting a nonprofit fellowship program with my wife. She smiled and assumed it was something I would eventually do. However, I got her attention when I told her my radical vision to take a sabbatical from my career and concentrate on launching the CL Thomas Fellowship full-time. I was serious about making this group as memorable and meaningful as possible, at least for a dedicated period of time. She was on board—as long as the work sabbatical ended before we ran out of money. I accepted those very reasonable terms and pressed on with planning the fellowship!

In the wake of the sudden loss of my father, I had to face it: What did I want to accomplish professionally in my life? What would be my legacy? Would I just go home and carry on with business as usual? I picked up a copy of the toast I gave about Pop. I had been able to see so clearly what Pop stood for and the legacy he had left for me. I believed the fellowship was the answer and I just needed to put some more thought and planning around the launch. I was confident I would figure out the career question. I believed the fellowship deserved my full attention.

This is what led me to utter the words at the beginning of this chapter: "I'm resigning as CEO."

Up until this point, I had experienced all the highs and lows of running a small business. It was a wild ride from cash flow crunches, hires, fires, and the thrill of winning big contracts. However, I felt that my time was coming to an end as I kept thinking about coaching and mentoring others through the fellowship. I had served as a "bridge CEO" to give the founder a well-deserved break, and now that he was rejuvenated, he was the best person to lead the company again. I prayed for wisdom on my next steps.

Although the timing felt right, I didn't want to rush any decisions. After all, this job was providing for my family! How ironic would it be to mentor others on how to provide when I had no job! I smiled to myself; it was all so crazy. They (whoever "they" are) say you shouldn't make any significant changes in life for at least a year after a close family member or friend dies.

For me, this was not a knee-jerk decision, rather a calling that I could not shake—my own version of a "Personal Legend." Plus, the grieving book Mom bought me had advised that each of us handle seasons differently. So rather than staying in my room to wait out the cold winter days, I was, in a sense, eager to get out in the snow to explore what I could discover on the snow-capped mountains.

It would not be easy yet it would be worth the polar plunge, and I was taking bold action in my career. Could I leverage all the self-development work I had done for the benefit of others? Could I discover a sustainable way to provide for my family in the process?

To help me consider this decision, I met with one of my mentors, Tim. We met at a local rooftop bar. I walked just a few blocks from my office, yet the city looked so different from this perspective. It was an appropriate setting as I shared my new views on life and work. This was the first time I was articulating the vision for the fellowship outside of my immediate family.

We were the only people sitting on the rooftop this particular morning, which fostered an intimate discussion about finances, faith, and how to grieve well. When I started to go into more details of my plan to leave work and focus on launching the fellowship, his eyes narrowed to focus on what I was saying. I could sense he, with his CFO background, was concerned about my plan. He actively listened before responding.

He looked at me and directly asked if I had prepared financially for such a bold decision. It was a great question that many friends and family members wouldn't have the courage to ask. Did it take the wind out of my sails a little bit? Yes. But that is precisely why I consult mentors like Tim on important matters before I act—I sometimes need a voice of caution.

I told him that I had enough savings to last until the end of the year before needing to dip into investments and retirement funds. The clock was ticking. I told Tim that I planned to focus on launching the fellowship first and then pursue new work. It sounded simple enough:

1. Start the fellowship group in the fall.
2. Then pursue a new career that challenged me and supported the family by the end of the year.

I was feeding off of the energy from the call with Matt, the marker-board moment, and the surprising word of fellowship. After explaining my plan to Tim (if you can call it that—more like a hope and a prayer!), he relaxed his piercing eyes and seemed satisfied with my time-line that I had just made up on the spot.

"Would this plan really work?" I thought to myself as I walked back from the meeting with my mentor.

————

A month later, I was offering a toast again, but this time it was to my former colleagues. It was my final day as their CEO.

By this point, everyone knew my vision for the CL Thomas Fellowship program. My business partners and colleagues stared back at me with a mixture of surprise and curiosity as we spent one last happy hour together as work colleagues.

Everything with the transition went smoothly, and I was even surprised on my last day to have the founder of the company fly in from out of state to see me off in style. He was showing his full support in a way that I truly appreciated. What a gesture! I had the support of my wife, my soon-to-be former colleagues, and my mentors. I had no idea what the future would hold for the fellowship or me, but I was ready!

So here I was, having just resigned my position as CEO to focus on launching the fellowship. I couldn't imagine anything more important to do with my time than take a leap of faith into the unknown and start a nonprofit mentoring program around this theme of becoming a provider. Some people were worried about me. It didn't matter, I was committed to this work and plan. At the same time, I don't want to discount the significance of this decision or suggest it is appropriate for everyone just to quit their job and start a nonprofit. Yet, the transition was the right move for me at the proper time. I felt I had given myself enough time and space to make this bold move.

It was time to develop the program, recruit guys into the first group, and discover a new satisfying career. Easy . . . until it wasn't.

Fall came, and I was supposed to launch the first fellowship group. I thought back to how confident I had felt with Tim at the rooftop bar when I first shared my plan. Well, I was now officially behind schedule and I needed to face this harsh reality.

I started this journey praying that the fellowship program would outlive me and provide for many lives. Now I was praying it wouldn't end before it even began! I had to keep practicing praying to remind myself to trust God. After all, God had given me the word *fellowship*, and so God had a plan with this adventure that was larger than mine. Right?

I had no job, my runway was expiring, and I didn't have a single recruit for the CL Thomas Fellowship.

Surprisingly, these separate challenges worked together to produce an unexpected solution.

To help improve recruitment efforts for the men's fellowship group, I decided to make a video introducing and promoting the opportunity.[1] My mentor, Tim, was back supporting me again. This time, rather than talking at a rooftop bar about my finances, he was donating his time to be part of the marketing video.

Finally, the applicants started coming in with only two weeks before the launch date! And the coolest part? *Exactly seven guys signed up.* Seven excellent referrals from personal and professional connections formed an outstanding group—perfectly representing those seven months of focused prayer and planning. What a joy to start! There was real work to be done now of actually leading the inaugural group.

Not only did my marketing efforts pay dividends for the fellowship, they unexpectedly opened up my career path. During the filming, Tim shared his personal experience with health coaching and the immense value he received by completing the training and certification program. As the videographer captured B-roll footage, I was collecting inspiration for my next career.

I went from scribbling gibberish on the notebook for the sake of acting in the video to feverishly taking notes on what Tim was saying. This all sounded interesting.

I had never even heard of health coaching or integrated medicine, let alone considering a career transition into the health and wellness industry. I was open to all possibilities, so I scribbled down *health coaching, Duke Integrative Medicine*.[2] Through some follow-up investigation work, I learned that this program taught active listening skills and asking powerful questions to help clients make positive behavioral changes. I believed these could all contribute to the fellowship group and perhaps my next career.

At this point, I didn't even understand what health coaching was but I applied for the program (after all, my calendar was wide open) and the next week I was accepted! Once again, I had no idea what I was doing, just following the momentum and good omens as they appeared —but I would soon face some obstacles along the way.

I went to pay for the program during the early-bird discount period and discovered I was too late. The class was at capacity and no longer accepting students! How could this happen? I was not only expecting a slot, but a discount for paying within the early bird window. My pride even had me thinking that I would be a "gift" to the class based on my business management experience. Now they didn't even have space for me. After getting excited about this opportunity, the door seemed to have shut abruptly. The good omen had turned evil on me! The program didn't have a slot for me, and I had no backup plans.

For the first time since being a college student, I had complete flexibility in my schedule, yet I wasn't sure what to do with it. During my time as CEO, I learned that it pays to be *pleasantly persistent* in both sales and hiring. I implemented this strategy upon the staff at Duke

Integrative Medicine for the health coaching training program. I contacted the program manager weekly, by e-mail or phone, asking for a slot. I politely and consistently reminded them it was likely now or never for me to complete this training program.

Eventually, another student dropped out once the final payment was due, and guess who was on top of the waitlist? I signed up immediately, this time as a grateful student versus an entitled former small-business CEO. This would not be the last time health coaching provided a humbling opportunity for my personal and professional growth.

I thoroughly enjoyed my training during the first semester, and then it was time to get real and actually coach clients during the second semester. I could also use these sessions as credit hours towards my national board certification. So, I offered free health coaching and started to add some clients thanks to some willing friends. While this was rewarding work, I wasn't making money and I was running out of my end-of-year financial runway. Just at that moment, another mentor breathed life into my career.

My mentor, Henry, and I had arranged a call, and since we didn't talk often, I wanted to maximize our conversation. He was in the private equity world and had plenty of connections with business leaders. My plan was to offer his investment companies free health coaching services. I thought giving away more free services would lead to paid engagements. I realize now this was a flawed plan because I was operating out of fear of rejection, but I didn't see this truth at the time. Instead, I told myself, "With more references, I can gain more credibility which will attract paying clients."

Henry answered the phone and I immediately went into my polished pitch. *Man, I nailed it!* I thought to myself. His response indicated otherwise.

"You have to provide for your family, right?"

Naturally, the word *provide* hit me in the gut with the strength of a heavyweight boxer. Here I was thinking I am a provider expert, starting a fellowship program and mentoring group around this theme, only to have a mentor call out the obvious—how are you going to financially provide? This is a sign of a true mentor, but I wasn't at a place to appreciate that in this particular moment.

"Well, yes," I said in response. "I do need to provide more financially for my family."

It wasn't only Henry's strategic use of the word *provide* in his comments, it was his perfect delivery. He was stating this truth in love. After his words sunk in, I knew he was right. I had already achieved enough credit hours for certification, and it was indeed time to transition from "this is *free*" to "this is worth your financial investment" to clients.

While I was still mentally reeling on the ropes, Henry interjected by asking how much my services cost. True to the theme of my life and career at that time, I made something up on the spot with no idea what I was doing.

He then said, "OK, I know what I am going to do." I wasn't sure what that meant either, but obviously, I wasn't coming up with a better plan. I thanked him and we ended the call. It was short and sweet, in a getting-hit-by-a-verbal-jab sort of way. I was curious what he was going to do next.

The next day, Henry posted a message on his personal LinkedIn account. It remains one of the most thoughtful and unexpected things anyone has ever said about me.

I love Justin. Super guy. Very intentional. Great heart. Been a successful entrepreneur and then after an experience with coaching, decided to hang up a shingle as a coach. He's just getting going and offering up really, really affordable rates and beard-growing tips. If I was 10 years younger, I'd sign up in a heartbeat.

With that gift, I got my first handful of paying clients! More importantly, I regained my confidence. Henry's words changed my career trajectory, the fellowship, and my provider journey.

For me, Henry's advice and endorsement was Proverbs 18:21 in action: "Death and life are in the power of the tongue." He believed in me and gave my career vision life, just when it needed to get off the mat.

You would think I had run out of mentors by now, but fortunately, I had another one just as the clock was ticking down on the calendar year. After Tim had introduced me to health coaching, and Henry introduced me to paying clients, I had the confidence to reach out to a mentor I hadn't connected with in years. And I was planning on boldly asking for a job. I wanted to fulfill my promise to my wife and myself that I would have a new clear direction with my career before the year ended.

This former boss and mentor was Dr. William "B.J." Lawson. He had recently co-founded dooable health, a company committed to making healthier workforces and helping employees need less healthcare through personal health coaching. This seemed to match my business background with new health coaching credentials, but I had learned to be humble throughout this new journey and wrote him the following e-mail on December 23, 2018:

Hi BJ!

Justin Thomas here. I joined your previous tech start-up back in 2006 as a Client Relations Team and am now a Health Coach. I recently completed the Duke Integrative Medicine Health Coach Foundation Training Program and started my own practice.

I came across your business, dooable health, and was pleasantly surprised you have a team of Health Coaches! I'd love to reconnect in the New Year to learn what you are doing and see if I can help in any way.

Merry Christmas,

Justin

To my delight, B.J. remembered me and responded on Christmas Eve, and we scheduled a coffee chat for January. I would eventually join his team and become a partner in the growing business.

Bold changes allowed me to experience new adventures during this season. I was running the fellowship, was a newly minted health coach, and back in leadership at a start-up in my new health and wellness field. This was all positive, but I was also struck with how things matter more to us when they cost us something.

I would not have started the CL Thomas Fellowship if I didn't lose my father. I would have never become a National Board-Certified health and wellness coach, or become a partner at the dooable health team if I didn't step into the unknown. The provider journey has cost me financially, and even more challenging, it has cost me my pride over and over, but it always leads to exciting new adventures.

CHAPTER SUMMARY

KEY TAKEAWAYS

- **Act boldly**: After a time of reflection, take action when you are ready, not when others tell you it is the right time. Only you know the calling on your life.
- **Trust your mentors by sharing your needs**: Speaking with a partner, mentor, friend, trusted boss, or colleague can be helpful in clarifying your next bold step.
- **Be pleasantly persistent**: Deciding to act boldly is often followed by a commitment over time in order to see your vision to reality.

CHALLENGE

What bold change do you need to make in your life? You have put in the time to reflect; now what courageous action do you need to take?

1. See the finished video at https://www.clthomasfellowship.org/ thanks to my friends at StoryDriven in Durham, NC for the great work!
2. For those interested in exploring health coaching training I recommend the Duke program, learn more at https://dhwprograms.dukehealth.org/health-wellbeing-coach-training/

CHAPTER 5

Create a Provider Vision

looked down at my watch—7:30 p.m. I looked back up to see four men staring at me when there should have been seven. The guys knew what was coming next. Push-ups!

We were halfway through the inaugural CL Thomas Fellowship. Everything had gone great, and up until this point, we had perfect attendance at our monthly meetings. I had a motivated, bright, and eager group of men in the fellowship. We had been reading books, memorizing Scripture, having lunch-and-learn sessions with some of my mentors, and undertaking various self-development challenges to help us become providers. However, this month—exactly halfway through—we had some missing in action, not just one or two, but *three*! This is no big deal for most groups, but those groups are not the CL Thomas Fellowship.

Part of the fellowship experience is agreeing to be present at the meetings unless providentially hindered. I know this may sound intense, and it is. It's a test to see how the men honor their commitments. Things will come up in life. That is what happened to a few of the fellowship guys this night. They had real challenges ranging from car issues to work responsibilities, yet the covenant was still broken. When covenants are broken, so is trust, and amends must be made.

We pay our debt in the fellowship through push-ups.

After completing my health coaching certification, I wanted to explore integrating a physical fitness component to the fellowship experience. Push-ups seemed to be a good idea! Plus, I had memories chiseled into my psyche from my intense (and loving) high school basketball coach who also effectively used them as motivation to arrive at practice on time.

Perhaps I was using too much positive psychology here from my health coach training, but I thought doing some push-ups was just the logical next step to take to keep our bar high in the fellowship.

The guys were not considering all of this when I told them to grab a spot on the carpet. They groaned at what they knew was coming. Amends needed to be paid before we could discuss the provider theme of the night.

I counted out twenty-five reps, and then we paused to recover before completing another twenty-five push-ups. The room was silent, just the heavy breathing that comes from abrupt and unexpected exercise. The men had come for tea and a comfortable seat on my sofa to explore our book and theme. Comfort could wait, and we finally completed our final set of twenty-five push-ups to honor the three missing brothers.

"Guys, we are entering the third quarter," I said as we settled into my office together after completing the seventy-five push-ups. "Just like in a race or game, this is the hardest part. We've completed half of the fellowship, and there is more to go. The first quarter of any new activity or commitment like this tends to be exciting. You start with all the promises and possibilities of an unknown adventure. The second quarter of that journey allows you to settle in and create some group norms. The third quarter, where we are now, is what gets most of us. It's easy to become tired from the first half of the journey. You look ahead, but can't see the end in sight yet. You have to choose if it's worth continuing. You just need to get through this third quarter so that you make it to the fourth quarter, where adrenaline takes over, and the end is in sight. What are we going to do?"

Of course, I was saying this to the guys that made it to the meeting, and I would soon share a similar message to the men who were not present. It's important as a leader to demonstrate you have standards and to address things immediately. Unfortunately, I needed to re-learn this leadership lesson in a future fellowship group where I did not address a member head-on and it resulted in the overall group suffering. Now I know that if the standards are not being met, the individual member needs to know and fix it or accept help to resolve the error. This is both a leadership and provider challenge.

We all have to find our own authentic style of blessing and protecting others. Push-ups were my strategy. Why push-ups? It's not because I want the most muscular group of men in my fellowship. It's because of what I've learned about the truth of being a provider. Providing requires presence and pain. I wanted to protect them from laziness, from not finishing strong.

Retired Navy SEAL David Goggins put it best: "Life will always be the most grueling endurance sport and when you train hard . . . [you] find a way to move forward no matter what." (Goggins 256) Similarly, the provider makes a covenant to show up and finish strong. The question is simple yet difficult to keep: *Will you be there?* Being there means being fully present. It might look like being physically present, such as the men in the fellowship showing up for our monthly meeting. It requires us to be disciplined with time management. It demonstrates commitment and respect, especially when you get to the third quarter of a commitment!

Beyond just showing up, I want to acknowledge that becoming a provider is not the path of least resistance. Providing for yourself and others is difficult to balance. We all will struggle to find that appropriate level of investment in ourselves while serving others.

It's far easier to live a life simply receiving from others and fading into the background. However, stepping into the provider role has its own unique challenges. Since we have discussed how important it is to address issues directly, let's face some of these provider concerns in that spirit. Here are the top excuses that I personally uttered along my journey and which I hear from others on why they do not believe they can become a provider.

1. **I need to focus on myself first before providing.** We do need to focus on our personal growth, yet we are not trying to become stronger to look good in the mirror; we want to use our strength for others. We all need to focus on providing for ourselves *and* providing for others. That is the mark of a true provider, one who is strategically investing and providing for themselves to better bless and protect those in their lives.

2. **I don't have a lot of money, so I can't provide.** This sells the word *provider* so short it's painful to hear. Don't think of a provider as the 1950s dad figure bringing home a paycheck as the pinnacle of providing. Our baseline definition needs to change from bringing in the money to blessing and protecting. You know this by now, yet it bears repeating: Providing = Blessing + Protecting. Only a couple out of the eight provider characteristics (which we'll get to later) deal with finances. There are many more opportunities to bless and protect others beyond finances.

3. **I don't have a spouse/kids so I don't need to be a "provider" yet.** Have you ever needed a blessing or some protection in your life? I'm sure you have, regardless of your marital status! Why, then, do we believe the lie that providing is only for our spouse or kids? We absolutely want to and will provide for our family when the time comes. But, there are many others that God has put in our lives to bless and protect. Plus, if you are single, don't you want some practice before you lead a family?

4. **I'm not (spiritually/emotionally) mature enough to be a provider.** In order to grow and mature, you need to engage. Doing nothing is not going to build confidence or belief that you are ready to provide. We need to resist the lie

that "When I feel more mature, I can provide more." It's similar to sports. You don't just wait around until you have matured into an all-star to start playing the game. You put in the work and build the skills to become the best version of yourself. We all start out as a "rookie" provider, and we all have the opportunity to become a seasoned "veteran" provider that allows us to have more weight in our spheres of influence.

5. **I don't have a good example to follow.** One of the CL Thomas fellows remarked that there were very few examples of providers in his social circle. It was a sad yet honest assessment. He told me, "Yes, Jesus is an example of doing all of these perfectly, but there are not many men leading lives in this manner." Others state that they simply hadn't seen a solid provider (physically, emotionally, spiritually, financially, etc.) in life. This is a real barrier to overcome for a lot of people as it is a struggle to replicate something you haven't seen or experienced. Therefore, I hope this book serves as a practical resource to learn from and be inspired by along your journey, especially if you do not have strong provider examples in your life currently.

To help us overcome these common excuses, I believe having a compelling and authentic vision is essential. Motivation and willpower eventually fade (especially in the "third quarter," as discussed). We can envision our ideal future state while being brutally honest with where we are today. For instance, when you want to get out of debt, you first need to know how much debt you currently have so you can create a winning strategy. It sounds easy, but we tend not to take time to come up with an authentic personal development vision. I experienced an exercise that freaked me out around vision-setting in my health coach training program, but it was powerful and effective.

"Get into a comfortable position with both of your feet planted on the floor," the teacher instructed. I was sitting in a classroom with thirty-five fellow students at Duke Integrative Medicine. Classmates had flown in from all over the country, even from as far as Brazil and Israel, to attend our first week of training. I was impressed with the diversity of the class but I was beginning to feel slightly out of place—actually *really* out of place—with this meditation exercise.

I wanted practical tips and how-to guides on facilitating group discussions for my upcoming fellowship groups. And, honestly, I wanted the credibility of saying I was certified from Duke. My internal dialogue was interrupted as my teacher's instructions continued, "Allowing your eyes to close or cast down, begin to focus your awareness on your breath." Yup, I was now ready to leave. However, I stuck it out—after all, I had paid good money for this training and practically begged for the final slot!

The breathing exercise continued for another minute or two. When I was settling in, I heard further instructions: "Your future self is waiting for you, waiting to talk to you." I was the skeptic in the room during this exercise. I looked around to see if I could make eye contact with any other fellow cynics. Nothing.

All the other students seemed to be right in their yoga-loving position, ready for more. Once again, I reminded myself I paid to be here, so I gave it another shot. I listened intently and followed the cues of our instructor to begin to get into the flow of intentional breathing exercises. Then, something incredible happened. With my eyes closed, I remember seeing a clear picture of my future self. This weird health-coaching mojo was starting to work on me.

The teacher wrapped up the exercise. "When you open your eyes, please remain silent, pick up your paper and crayons, and begin drawing whatever you remember from this journey."

I did what I was instructed and started drawing the image I saw in my head. My future self was an endurance athlete that seemed surprisingly like a seasoned military veteran.

I had no intention of really transitioning from my civilian life to a military career. Plus, simulating drowning and lack of sleep are not my top desires. However, the image represented strength and confidence that had been cultivated through earned experience, not passive living.

My future self was better than I was at the moment. He was willing and able to protect those around him from harm with bold words and confident actions. This future self was not soft nor timid, yet still offered *tender strength*. I felt at ease and inspired by the projected future image of myself. I was not overwhelmed or intimidated by him; it was me, just a stronger version. I couldn't believe the exercise prompted such a clear vision and I felt far away from achieving this.

I would soon test how far this provider vision could take me.

I believe vision is at the center of becoming a provider. In later chapters, we will discuss all the different habits, but I'd like to leave you with this visual as you reflect on how you would begin to describe your own vision at the center of your journey.

THE PROVIDER WHEEL

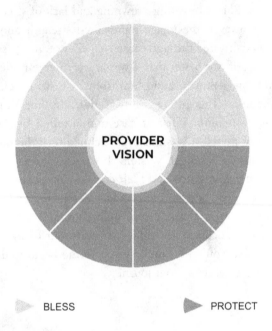

PROVIDER VISION

BLESS   PROTECT

———————— CHAPTER SUMMARY ————————

KEY TAKEAWAYS

- **Prepare for the third quarter grind:** Excitement wears off. When it's just as easy to turn back as it is to push forward, you need encouragement and a clear vision of the "why" to press to the end.
- **Direct communication is required to hold standards:** If something is important, it's worth a hard conversation.
- **Visioning can make you uncomfortable**: Whether you are in a classroom setting or in the privacy of your home, visioning your future may feel awkward and that is often where growth happens.

CHALLENGE

What is your provider vision? What does it feel like to be at your best for others? You may be pleasantly surprised to learn that you can visualize your future self through a visioning exercise, give it a try!

CHAPTER 6

Overcome Obstacles

Motivated by my new provider vision, I signed up for a GoRuck Tough challenge. This is an overnight 10-12-hour, team-based endurance event led by former and current military Special Operations professionals for regular civilians like me. It seemed like a good idea at the time . . .

You just sign up and show up carrying a backpack with thirty pounds of steel, plus any food, water, and essentials to get you through. The military operations leader, or "cadre," also brings a plethora of extra weight that the team has to carry throughout the night, such as sandbags, water jugs, and logs while completing specific assigned tasks. Did I mention you pay for this experience? Crazy, I know! There seemed to be a theme in my life of paying for activities that seemed ridiculous.

On top of all this craziness, there is no winner. The goal is to finish as a team and endure whatever exercises and "missions" the cadre presents. In the end, everyone receives a patch to commemorate the experience. Today, I've inched toward my future version of myself by completing over a dozen of these events. Although I received a patch at each one, my contribution level has varied drastically. I'm still a long way from that seasoned and confident future version of myself, but I am actively growing into him.

During my first GoRuck Tough challenge, I was scared to death.

My future version was not looking like a reality any time soon! I had no idea what I was doing or really why I signed up. Even after my inspirational vision exercise, I was insecure about what I could contribute to this team event. The event started at 9 p.m., and darkness surrounded me as I anxiously awaited starting instructions from the cadre along with my other teammates.

Everyone was silent. I could feel the nervousness swell inside of me. I positioned myself at the back of the line as much as possible and didn't talk. In preparation for this 12-hour challenge, I even bought an old hockey practice shirt to provide an extra cushion underneath all my layers of clothing.[1] Imagine an athletic short-sleeve shirt but with shoulder and chest padding. I was worried about my body not being able to handle the load of the event. I thought this hack would work. Unfortunately, it didn't save my shoulders; nothing would have. Plus, I looked ridiculous, more like the Bubble Boy in the infamous Seinfeld episode rather than a strong competitor. Not a good start.

The event began with some basic physical training drills. As I was swinging my rucksack during an exercise, I noticed something spewing out of my bag. My water bladder had sprung a leak with all the swinging! As I completed rep after rep, I viewed in terror as my life source, my packed water, wasted away in front of my shell-shocked eyes! This was getting worse and worse, and we had just started. Mercifully the warm-up exercises finished before all of my water spewed out. We then moved into team drills where things did not get any better as I discovered there was a basement to my current rock-bottom feelings.

Out of thirty guys, the cadre pointed to me and said, "You are in charge." This was not my idea of fun. *Why did I do this again?* The cadre quickly explained that I needed to organize my team over an obstacle while only having three shoes touching the ground at any given time in a designated area.

I became utterly unraveled and stood frozen in silence. I was running the cadre's instructions through my head, hoping for a brilliant strategy to appear suddenly. Unfortunately, I was nowhere close to my vision of a strong, capable leader who could be trusted. My team realized I was worthless and defaulted to a mob mentality by literally pushing me out of the way and taking turns shouting instructions. Not surprisingly, we failed to complete the challenge and had to do some penalty exercises. I had failed.

I quickly returned to the comfort of the shadows. With the familiar feeling of passiveness, I was back at home. The event carried on and the cadre brought us to a spot with some "presents." Unfortunately, this was no Christmas morning gift exchange. Instead, I saw two massive logs and a "regular" log. The large ones required three to four guys to carry it on their shoulders and the regular log only needed a couple of guys. I tried to muster up the strength from my happy place of being a spectator, but it was short-lived. I started out under the big log thinking my hockey shirt was going to support it. Nope, I literally got crushed.

Doing my best to go unnoticed, I started dropping the idea of achieving my future self-vision and shrank again to the back of the line until I got out of the log-carrying rotation entirely. My shoulders were burning from pain. I couldn't imagine lifting those logs.

Over ten hours later, we were still competing in the event. We had gone through the night; the sun was now up and the end in sight. We had about a mile left to go and they needed a "casualty"—someone to play hurt and be carried to the finish line. As one of the smaller guys on the team, I gladly volunteered. To add insult to injury, just as we were about to cross the finish line, the guy carrying me spun around to look back at our group and my face slammed into another teammate's weight plate. I had made it 10+ hours without a serious injury, and then with ten minutes remaining, my eye was swollen shut from the impact. It would become an impressive black eye after the event, and when friends would ask how I got the shiner, I was forced to relive the spectator moment.

From this example, you can tell I was not in the mindset of blessing or protecting anyone other than myself. I was too fearful, timid, and weak (mentally and physically) to contribute to the overall group. I tried to do my part but I was exposed as a worthless teammate. I was operating out of a selfish and passive mentality—it was all about me and protecting myself. Even from the beginning, I was focused on becoming the endurance athlete but not once considering the needs around me.

We are not called to fade in the background just because it feels safe. I knew I could do better, be better. So I vowed never to use that hockey shirt again and to get stronger for the next event.

The GoRuck event showed me how it's not about shining bright for a moment. I hadn't shone at all during my first couple of events! I kept trying to contribute to these crazy challenges but kept falling short, always at the rear of the pack. These endurance challenges required me to persevere through the night and its seemingly endless challenges. I realized it was not just physically challenging, but also required a great deal of mental fortitude—an area that I had not spent time working on. I needed to build myself up from the ground up, physically and emotionally. It was time to take an honest look at my strengths and weaknesses.

First, I realized I had become comfortable based on growing up as a big fish in a small pond. I attended a small Christian school where leadership positions were offered to everyone. I was Romeo in the school play, president of my class, and captain of the basketball team. Seeing the success of this strategy, I attended a small liberal arts college which also afforded plenty of opportunities. I was elected president of my business fraternity as only a sophomore, and later served as large-group coordinator for the Christian student group. All of these positions put me "on stage" and in front of people. I wasn't that big of a fish, but the pond was nice and small, and I could be easily noticed.

As life progressed, I continued to find myself being the face of organizations and teams. My first job out of college was training physicians. Later, during my MBA program, I looked forward to presentations so much that I made side bets with one of my classmates that I could take whatever word or phrase he gave me just minutes before my presentation and incorporate it in seamlessly.

One time he gave me the word "angels," which was challenging, but I made it into the presentation with the ridiculous line of: "This is a proven process, and when we implement and experience how smoothly the supply chain functions, it will feel as if angels are singing, and it will bring peace of mind to management." Like I said, I lived for the stage.

I have to admit this is where my father and I differed. He knew true character is built on integrity. He knew *integrity* was quiet and authentic and hated the spotlight. He showed me it was developed off the grid.

I have had to learn the value of integrity the hard way. Having the constant experience of being in front of people, whether facilitating meetings or formally presenting, I developed some positive characteristics, but they also had some unintentional consequences. I started to discount experiences that did not help me get recognition. I would work tirelessly on "spotlight" activities such as presentations, speeches, and planning big events. However, the motivation to do the mundane or background work never made it on my priority list. This was why I struggled so mightily during endurance events; I struggled to labor on when a commitment to the mundane was required for success.

One night, I was washing the dishes when this lesson of honoring the behind-the-scenes moments of life finally hit me. Ever since I heard that word "fellowship" from God, I've tried to tune into and become more sensitive to these gentle nudges and omens. Rather than focusing my thoughts on being "the guy," I needed not just to serve more, but also to serve *joyfully*. In addition, I realized that I wasn't just training to be a better teammate in the GoRuck Challenge, but to become a better husband and father to my family.

Every night I had an opportunity to do the dishes for our family. It was an opportunity to demonstrate "GoRuck mental toughness" in doing something I didn't necessarily want to do, but that it could help me *develop the habit* of joyfully serving others and persevering when no one was looking. That's integrity. There would be no prize or celebration of my achievement. This dish washing work not only forged my mind to become mentally stronger to push through endurance challenges, but to better serve my family in the process. That is the ultimate goal of the journey—to provide for ourselves in order to serve others better.

By committing to turn the mundane into the memorable, I realized we don't require a date night with our spouse to have fun. We can have valuable time by serving one another with activities like washing the dishes while engaging in thoughtful conversation. Don't get me wrong, my wife and I still have fun adventures together and meaningful moments outside of the kitchen, but I needed to start seeing all the life opportunities to serve her and our family beyond the "spotlight" moments.

I was trying to exorcise my demons of desiring the spotlight, one dish at a time. As each plate got washed, I was making progress. My mental challenge was to put the same effort into cleaning up as I did on polishing that perfect pitch. The challenge was real. I did not start with the right attitude, but at least I started. Eventually, my perspective caught up to my behavior. For once, I was genuinely serving with a joyful heart—all thanks to some dishes. Without realizing it, I was becoming stronger for my next GoRuck challenge through this daily chore.

In *The Four Loves*, C. S. Lewis talks about not only imitating Christ at Calvary, but also imitating Christ in the everyday busyness of life. "Our model is the Jesus, not only of Calvary, but of the workshop, the roads, the crowds, the clamorous demands and surly oppositions, the lack of all peace and privacy, the interruptions. For this, so strangely unlike anything we can attribute to the Divine Life in itself, is apparently not only like, but is the Divine Life operating under human conditions." (Lewis 7)

I now aspire to imitate Christ in the mundane, everyday moments. One dish at a time.

We had endured the third quarter together, and now the inaugural CL Thomas Fellowship was coming to a close. I had a special surprise for the fellows. Instead of the usual meeting in the living room, I invited them outside to the fire pit. We had completed nine months of rigorous assignments. They thought the new meeting location was the surprise, and we started as normal, reciting our memory verses and talking about the assigned book.

Then, instead of continuing with our standard fellowship meeting agenda, I paused and told them I had a gift for them.

I lifted a large box onto the table with the GoRuck logo displayed. I told the guys in the fellowship that I wanted to share my provider story through my experience with the GoRuck challenge and give them a token of that journey to carry with them as a symbolic representation of our time together.

As I shared with you, I described my first few failures during these endurance events, and then there was a turning point. I turned to the men to share more.

I told them that during the latest challenge, I went from a silent participant to a more confident and engaged one, encouraging teammates by sharing strategies for carrying logs and sandbags. In addition, I was taking lessons from the dishes and serving others. The funny thing was this event was like my disastrous first one in many ways. It had the exact weight requirement, time duration, and rules. However, I had carried a provider mindset from start to finish.

How?

I had been more intentional in my training leading up to the event, and my mental state had also improved. I had provided for myself to be able to serve others during the event. Rather than just being consumed with my shoulders and my pain, I raised my strength, which allowed me to see my teammates for the first time. For instance, when a fellow participant needed an assistant, he chose me, someone he could trust to do whatever needed to be done.

I looked back and continued sharing with the men of the fellowship and how at the end of this latest grueling 12-hour event, our cadre made the dreaded announcement that one of our other teammates was a "casualty" and needed to be carried to the finish line.

At this moment during the challenge, we all stopped, feeling more exhausted based on this news. Everyone took a moment to catch our breath and complain. We were all on fumes. Feet blistered, shoulders chafed, and the heat of the morning starting to increase—someone needed to carry this teammate.

To everyone's surprise—including my own—I stepped up and slung the guy across my shoulders and walked onward. No words spoken, just action taken. Then, when I didn't think I had anything to give, I reached deeper.

That is the provider mentality. I didn't get there the first time. Remember how I volunteered to be carried by someone else during my first challenge? Now I was lifting this teammate (albeit just a few blocks) to kickstart our group again.

I should mention that I'm just an average guy. I reach 5'10" if I have the right shoes on. I weigh 165 pounds with the right clothes on. I am not the Incredible Hulk; I'm just a regular guy. And I picked up that teammate and carried him as far as I could. My action inspired the rest of the team because I looked so "regular." They followed me and then others took turns carrying our fallen comrade.

After we crossed the finish line and received our event patch, one of my teammates came straight over to me with intensity in his eyes. He was still riding high on adrenaline from the event and the thrill of being done—finally! He put his arm around me and said, "Dude, you are a badass. You're skinny but strong. I couldn't believe you picked up that guy."

Let me tell you, it is so much more rewarding being strong enough to carry someone else (and being called a badass was kind of cool, I will admit). It took time, training, and a change in attitude.

After sharing this story with the fellowship guys, I started to open the box I had set before them. I told them that similar to my experience doing GoRuck challenges, we are all being challenged with opportunities to provide for ourselves to serve others better. The question is, are you preparing to be the one to carry someone when they need you to shoulder their burdens? Are you working on developing your strengths for the benefit of others? Or are you happy collecting "badges" in life just for your glory?

I told the men I wanted to give them their own GoRuck rucksack. It represented my journey of moving from selfishness and passiveness to an active participant trying to become a better version of myself for others.

I wanted to give them my best during the fellowship, and more importantly, I wanted to equip them to become providers. So I called up each guy individually and spoke a quick word of encouragement and blessing over them as I gave each their own bag. There was a custom patch attached to the backpack with the CL Thomas Fellowship logo to commemorate their accomplishment of completing the program.

We huddled around the fire pit as the night closed in, reflecting on the journey together. I remember the feeling of special moments with Pop where you felt close to him without needing any words, just being present in the moment. I had that same warmth now being around these men who had become like brothers. They joked, "Justin, you may have better fellowship classes, but we will always be the first!"

We enjoyed some belly laughs together, and I just soaked it all in. We all had further to go to become the provider God wanted us to be. Still, I was confident the fellowship had helped us all start the journey with a new passion and intentionality that did not previously exist in our lives. The vision of the CL Thomas Fellowship had become a reality.

I'm glad I listened to that voice in the shower that dropped the word "fellowship" seemingly out of nowhere. I needed to grow in my role as a provider on short notice for my family. I love sharing everything I have with the men of the fellowship. The best of Pop's life lessons, the Scriptures that challenge my thinking, the mentors who shaped my career, and my resources to help the men experience biblical generosity. The great part is that it's not just *my* calling. We are all invited to this provider adventure.

The GoRuck challenge is an event. There are lots of great lessons to be learned during the event, but it always ends. The journey of being a provider is a grand adventure that never ends. Being a provider is a weighty call throughout a lifetime. You can develop into a trusted provider who is equipped to consistently bless and protect others. We can all be that person who makes a positive difference, who provides for him or herself to ultimately build others up.

GoRuck has a motto of "SEEK PAIN." Here is how they describe this life philosophy on the website:

> The choice you have is whether you retreat toward the sirens of a comfortable life, always at the mercy of uncontrollable forces—or whether you harden your resolve and lead an empowered life. To SEEK PAIN is our way of life no matter the circumstances that we choose or that choose us. Therein lies the growth, and the meaning, and the purpose for all the days of our lives.

Let's not lag in the back of the pack hoping to be carried through life. Get in the game—join the invitation to grow your provider muscles. It may hurt like those logs, but you will be ready to lift up others when it's time.

CHAPTER SUMMARY

KEY TAKEAWAYS

- **Having a vision doesn't mean you won't be scared:** While having a clear vision is a great first step, implementing your provider vision will likely include times of uncertainty, and even some fear.
- **We are not called to fade in the background just because it feels safe:** Challenges such as the GoRuck endurance events expose our weaknesses and show us where

we can and need to grow to be more active participants and to provide beyond ourselves.

- **Train not just for special events but for everyday life**: While events are great motivators to improve, people matter over the events. Ensure that all the training is allowing you to serve the important relationship in your life.

CHALLENGE

What could you be building in your life right now that is worth the inevitable obstacles? Consider taking on a new challenge that would strengthen your provider muscles to carry someone's burden.

---

1. Here is what these padded shirts look like https://www.purehockey.com/c/hockey-protective-padded-shirts

CHAPTER 7

Our Turn to Provide

To be the provider, you simply need to provide. However, I learned firsthand how difficult this is when trying to implement it in real life. So, I set out to explore and test this theory of trying to provide for others intentionally. I had invested in myself through my sabbatical season, education, and training to become a health coach, and hours of intentional conversations with mentors, so, I was ready and eager to walk the walk and provide for someone in a meaningful way. It's an experiment filled with zest and awkward moments that I am sure will entertain and hopefully inspire you with positive momentum along your journey, without the clumsiness.

Before Pop passed away, my wife and I moved to the historic town of Hillsborough, NC. Pop was able to visit our new home shortly after our move, which is a fond memory. He asked how we liked the area during his trip and I told him I was getting involved in the community by starting a new F3 workout downtown.

F3 is an established community and there were workouts around my new hometown, but nothing in Hillsborough at the time. So I decided to start one! F3 describes itself as a "national network of free, peer-led workouts for men. We plant, grow, and serve these groups to invigorate male community leadership." That sounded like a great, real-life case study into becoming a provider.

Pop asked what F3 stood for and I told him it was for fitness, fellowship, and faith.[1] I was part of the team that helped establish and organize three workouts a week and a monthly happy hour. However, we weren't doing anything around the third *F*, the faith component. I continued being very involved in F3, not thinking about that third *F* until Pop passed. Then I came across a convicting Scripture in James 1:27, which reads: "Pure and genuine religion in the sight of God the Father means caring for orphans and widows in their distress and refusing to let the world corrupt you" (New Living Translation).

My heart broke as I realized my mom was now a widow. This passage in James motivated me to think of other people in need, specifically widows, who didn't have anyone in their lives to support them and who may need practical help. I had an idea.

At the next monthly F3 social, I brought up the concept of "adopting a widow" as part of our faith work in F3. We would serve a widow and help with whatever she needed. After all, we were men waking up early and working out at least three times a week. We were all in decent shape (or at least had a desire to get there!), which seemed to fit our mission. There was wholesale agreement amongst the group to give this idea a shot, so we just needed to find a widow.

I asked the men to send me recommendations and even e-mailed a couple of local pastors. Unfortunately, I didn't know of any widows in my neighborhood, and apparently, I was not alone. After this "brilliant idea," I had no leads until I met the "poodle-walkin' guy."

I decided to ruck (i.e. walk while wearing a weighted backpack) to and from the workout one morning. So I was walking back to my house, sporting a sweat-drenched outfit and a shovel flag, when the unexpected and divine meeting occurred. At every F3 workout site, a flag is attached to a shovel to indicate the starting point. Picture a tired, disheveled, bearded homeless-looking guy walking the streets with a flag and that was a pretty accurate image of how I must have looked on this particular morning after a challenging exercise session.

As I labored towards home, I saw a man walking his dog towards me. The man stopped dead in his tracks and asked, "What's your mission?" looking inquisitively at my American flag connected to a shovel.

I told the gentleman that I was part of a free men's workout group. Then I noticed he was wearing a t-shirt from a local church. It reminded me of James 1:27, and I told him about our "adopt a widow" idea. I mentioned we were looking for someone to serve in our area and asked if he knew of anyone. His eyes brightened up. He had just worked at a lady's home who was in need. I immediately took out my phone and asked for his contact information. Right there on the spot, I sent him an email and signed it "workout guy Justin" so that he could remember me and possibly share my contact information with the lady he had in mind.

A few hours later that day I received the following e-mail from him:

> Hello, Justin.
>
> A pleasure meeting you this morning! Wendy is the lady I met this week through work.
>
> She resides in an early 1990s-model doublewide. The yard needed some attention/maintenance, and her crawlspace needed work to keep out creatures.
>
> She expressed to me her financial woes due to poor health and extreme prescription drug cost. She would probably be receptive to your mission.
>
> Have a great day!
>
> Poodle-walkin' guy

I loved how he signed his email and how he kept referring to my mission. Being the provider does make life more exciting, as if we are on a secret and critical mission, challenging us to care for ourselves and others. His friendly gesture went above and beyond friendly salutations and description of my "mission." In addition, he broke several confidentiality rules of engagement by including Wendy's full contact information from his work database!

I don't want to get this guy fired, so I'm trying to keep details of his profession limited. The point here is that we both took a risk. I was bold enough to tell him about the adopting a widow "mission," and he was willing to provide a client who came to his mind. I finally had a lead. It felt like all of this was a divine meeting!

Then I did nothing.

A week or so later, I was sitting in my home office. I had an afternoon free of any client calls or pressing deadlines. Then I thought back to Wendy. I wanted to make sure this idea didn't continue to get lost in the noise of my life. I recognized that I wasn't taking action even though it was an important project, and I could meet a potential need. At that moment, for some reason, I thought the best and most practical thing to do was to drive to Wendy's house unannounced.

I know this sounds crazy, but I was afraid that I might lose motivation if I waited any longer and that Wendy wouldn't answer her phone or respond to an email from a stranger. Why I thought she would answer the door from a stranger is beyond me! I simply believed that I would have a better chance of meeting her in person.

I walked out of my home office and into the kitchen where my wife prepared lunch for our two young girls. I matter-of-factly asked her if I should wear a suit and tie since I was going to a lady's house unannounced. She naturally wanted more details regarding this idea before answering this peculiar question.

Amy emphatically stated that I would look like a cheesy salesman if I changed into a suit and went knocking on strangers' doors. She also said it was ridiculous that I was driving and not emailing or texting first. Fair point. Yet, I was undeterred and full of enthusiasm and I didn't want to lose the momentum that seemed to be pushing me forward at this moment. So I loaded up in my car, still wearing my casual t-shirt and shorts from my work-from-home wardrobe, and started driving to Wendy's house.

Fifteen minutes later, the GPS announced I had arrived. I was in the middle of a trailer park but I didn't see the house number I was looking for. I drove up and down, scouring the homes but had no luck finding Wendy's number. I then decided that I would go to the house closest to the GPS marker. It did not look welcoming. In fact, it was the worst home in the lot.

I drove past the "Do Not Trespass" signs and walked up the driveway. The steps and porch had lumber littered all on it. There were multiple cars broken down in the front lawn and a no-soliciting sign on the door. A lot of signs were telling me to stop, abort the mission! My zeal had not waned, however, so I pressed on; or rather I balanced as I placed my feet on some of the uneven stacks of lumber on the front porch and cautiously knocked.

No one came to the door. As I waited for the first time, my excitement meter started to drop. Perhaps this plan might have some strategic holes in it. Before I risked getting any trespassing charges levied against me, I left and headed quickly back to my car. Perhaps my wife was right, I may need to try calling Wendy.

Wendy's number went to voicemail and I proceeded to ramble on about who I was, what F3 was, our desire to help out, and to call back. I didn't feel confident she would return my call.

Before giving up, I wanted to try one more strategy. I would drive to a more welcoming-looking home, without all the "No Trespassing" signs, to ask if they knew Wendy. I located just the house across the street. As I pulled in, there was a car exiting the driveway and a lady walking beside it. I pulled over to allow space and then jumped out.

"Do you know Wendy?" I asked her.

"I'm Wendy," she replied.

"Great! I just left you a message."

The car paused beside us, and the older gentleman driver stared at me and back to Wendy. He (rightfully) looked suspiciously at me in my wannabe tech Silicon Valley entrepreneur outfit of tight V-neck t-shirt, shorts, and flip flops. Though I hadn't explained who I was or what I was doing, Wendy waved him on and said, "It's fine, you can go."

I thought this was strange, but the car and driver sped right on by!

I explained to Wendy that someone nominated her for a service project with my local workout group to provide for a neighbor. She looked surprised and said, "Oh, I thought you were with the roofing company to fix my roof." Of course, I laughed and told her I couldn't do that, especially not how I was dressed!

Fortunately, Wendy did not call the cops on me and we spent the next twenty minutes talking.

It was the beginning of a friendship. In our short introductory conversation together, I learned that Wendy had been the caretaker for her parents and then a friend with dementia who had all recently passed away. She had accumulated many of their material goods but didn't have the time or energy to organize it all. Wendy was overwhelmed and had all the inherited items hidden away in a storage unit. However, she could no longer afford the monthly storage costs and needed to move everything out by the end of the month. When I pulled up, she had just walked over to her neighbor's house to ask for his help.

After I heard this story and learned of this practical need, I could not contain my excitement.

"This is a divine meeting, Wendy!" I exclaimed. "Let's schedule a moving day!" Once again, it's amazing she did not call the police on me, especially after curiosity got the best of me when I tried "qualifying her" as a widow at one point, awkwardly asking, "So are you the only one in the house?"

Looking back, this was a poor question to ask. As I said, many things could have gone awry here—but I was becoming a provider one messy step at a time.

Next, I did what was the natural next step to solidify our friendship. We took a selfie together and hugged. We had adopted our "widow." That is what happens when you start engaging your provider muscle. You notice opportunities. You create opportunities. You bless and protect in ways you never expected.

A few weeks later, a dozen or so guys showed up and helped Wendy on moving day. She was elated—and so was her neighbor, who no longer had to be the one to carry all her stuff! The day was nearly a perfect success. The only casualty was my phone. The screen cracked after falling off a ladder as I yet again wanted a picture to remember this moment. The casualty of my phone's screen reminded me how moving from passive living to provider living can hurt sometimes. It costs us something to live for others. Most of the time it costs us our comfort. It's comfortable cruising through life, but that does not mean that is life-giving. I didn't care about the phone. In fact, I kept the crack for a few months just as a reminder of the cost of becoming a provider—and to remind myself to buy a better case next time.

At the end of the moving day, Wendy and I were standing outside her house. Her stuff was out of storage, and the guys had done an excellent job serving her well. It was a provider job well done. Wendy looked at me, and with tears forming in her eyes said, "You don't know how much this blessed me. Keep doing what you are doing; even if it doesn't always work out, you will be blessed."

Her remarks struck me so deeply that I immediately transcribed them on my phone when I got into my car. If I'd never taken a risk, if I'd never stepped outside of my needs, we would have never met Wendy or received the gift of blessing her. Would I have been motivated to try and adopt a widow without losing Pop and appreciating the challenges, hurts, and struggles of those around me? Sadly, probably not. I am grateful I woke up to this change of attitude and perspective. To remind me of the goal, I needed to create a visual guide, a simple yet powerful framework to force me out of my daily comfort and produce more memorable moments of provision.

THE BLESS & PROTECT MATRIX

After our successful experience with Wendy, I reflected on the primary drivers on what "being the provider" was and how best to demonstrate that visually. I had learned from Pop's letter and Psalm 23 that being a provider meant blessing and protecting others, as Jesus does for us. I asked myself: *If Jesus's provision is to bless and protect us, what does that look like in our lives?*

I then did what many MBA grads would do in this scenario—create a classic 2x2 matrix! This helped me explore the two key dimensions of providing for others through blessing and protecting. The matrix challenged me to evaluate which quadrants I naturally fell into as well as the opportunity for growth.

THE BLESS & PROTECT MATRIX

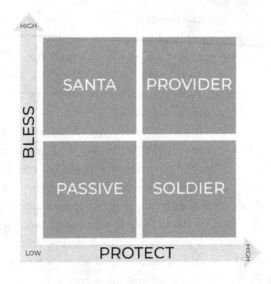

THE FOUR QUADRANTS

Lower Left: Passive

This is our default nature. We all start here and have to fight the constant pull back to the bottom left of the matrix. When we live in this "Passive" quadrant, we demonstrate low blessing and protecting characteristics in our lives. Individuals here are busy and active in life, but not living with intentionality. They think they are doing the best they can and simply feel there is no excess time, energy, or resources for themselves or anyone else. This mindset is a self-fulfilling prophecy and results in an inability to grow or help others. They might want to help others; they just don't believe they can bless or protect others at this moment.

Upper Left: Santa

As we progress up the matrix by improving our blessing habits, we enter into the "Santa" quadrant. This is where we are generous and kind, blessing people with gifts—just like Santa! However, when did Santa ever help you beyond a gift? Sometimes in life, we don't need a shiny new present; we need a strong hand of protection, perhaps even a hard truth spoken into our life. The Santa quadrant is fun to be in, to operate by solving problems and burdens through gifts. It's a safe place where we receive praise for apparent generosity. It's a fun quadrant to be in, both for the giver and receiver, yet there is a deeper version of providing. Blessing is only half of the role of the provider.

Lower Right: Soldier

For some of us, our first area of growth out of the passive quadrant is to be the "Soldier." We are high in the protecting trait but low in the blessing trait. We are a strong and reliable presence in someone's life through our prepared nature and foresight. We all need protectors in our lives. However, this is once again only half the role of the provider. The "Soldier" is not able to fully provide as people may be hesitant to be vulnerable and open to such a strong and stoic figure.

Upper Right: Provider

A well-developed leader has entered the "Provider" quadrant when they possess both a high degree of blessing and protecting characteristics. This is the most challenging and risky of all quadrants, for we must simultaneously exhibit "soft" and "hard" personalities, from tenderness to brute strength. From fun acts of generosity to the behind-the-scenes planning and work that builds the necessary character that may not be seen. This quadrant and role does not come naturally or easily and requires a variety of character strengths and habits to model the shepherd figure of Psalm 23.

The 2x2 matrix was a great start, but I wanted more clarity. I needed to know the specific traits that helped produce a high score on both the Bless and Protect axes. What specific habits would help me spend more time in the Provider quadrant? I will share these habits in greater detail over the following couple of chapters.

——————————————— CHAPTER SUMMARY ———————————————

KEY TAKEAWAYS

- **To be the provider, you need to provide**: This will be harder than it sounds, and it's part of the journey. Earnestly try to provide for yourself and then you will have the zest and excitement to find your own Wendy.
- **Embrace the messy journey**: You may discover bumps along the road of trying to develop the provider muscles. Be

kind to yourself and remind yourself that this is how growth happens; it's often uncomfortable and awkward, but there is fruit from all the effort!

- **We default to passiveness, but we don't have to stay there**: Becoming self-aware that this is our default posture allows us to improve how we bless and protect ourselves and others.

CHALLENGE

Who is one person that you can help this week? Once you discover that "provider energy," challenge yourself to pick one person and provide for what they need—better yet, recruit a group to help you make it happen!

---

1. See if there is an F3 near you by going to https://www.f3nation.com/

CHAPTER 8

The Blessing Habits

Remember that whiteboard brainstorming session I had when reflecting on the legacy of Pop's life in Chapter 4? Of all the positive habits and characteristic traits I saw in Pop's life, I wanted to distill the most impactful ones down to actionable items. Not only that, I wanted to try to avoid the inevitable risk of burnout from striving to achieve too many self-improvement projects at once.

Breaking down in front of my Pastor was good for my soul, but I arrived at that moment because I was serving others to exhaustion in the wake of Pop's death and had not appropriately provided for myself. Is there a way of blessing and protecting ourselves so we can do the same for others in a more sustainable way? This question led me back to the field of Integrative Medicine and my experience in health coaching.

Effective health coaching supports a client to consider their holistic health in order to maximize their well-being. Supporting clients in whatever area of health and wellness they desire to improve on by making lifestyle changes. The same is true for our provider journey. As we reviewed in Chapter 5, this journey starts by having an authentic vision and then we can decide where to start providing for ourselves in order to serve others.

Once again, I dusted off my MBA skills and put together a visual to represent how we are at our "provider best" when we are strong in all areas of blessing and protecting. The Provider Wheel was organized to make it easier to assess our current state of provision based on eight specific habits.

The top half of the Provider Wheel highlights the Blessing habits and the bottom presents the Protecting habits.

THE PROVIDER WHEEL

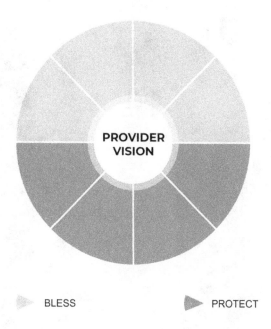

PROVIDER
VISION

▷ BLESS   ▶ PROTECT

We can't become someone new unless we try new things. We need to stop going with the flow of life and start making new positive waves in our lives and others along our path.

Let's start reviewing the top four blessing habits.

BLESSING HABIT #1: BE THERE

If we can't be there for ourselves and others, then this self-improvement exercise of becoming a provider is going to quickly fall flat. We simply have to show-up.

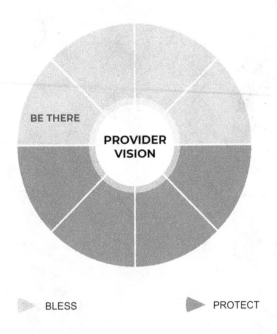

THE PROVIDER WHEEL

Showing up for ourselves might mean giving ourselves permission to take a nap when we are tired or reserving time on our calendars to just check-in with ourselves. Blessing ourselves and showing up for ourselves is the foundation for avoiding the risk of burn-out and chronic stress. Once we show-up for ourselves, we have the energy to be there for others.

Pop would take off for an annual hunting trip. I remember it would stress my Grandad out! Here was Mom with three kids living on the side of a mountain, 30-minutes from the closest town, and Pop was leaving her and the family to go horseback riding and hunting in places like Colorado, New Mexico, and even Alaska! Mom would always assure my Grandad she was fine. What she really meant was, I'll be fine because I know my husband needs this to be a better husband and father!

And true to form, his hunting adventures gave Pop a new sense of energy that he brought back to the family. After each trip, he would share tales from the drama of driving horses 2,000 miles in his trailer or the exciting stories of seeing animals in the wild during early morning hunts in the Rocky Mountains. As an added bonus, we were often given some new jerky from his more successful trips!

Both my parents were great examples of being there for us kids growing up and I was fortunate enough to see how they supported one another when they needed their own space. We have to be there for ourselves so we can keep showing-up for others. Part of the challenge is admitting our limitations regarding how many people we can really be there for based on our unique personalities.

For instance, early in their marriage, Mom would introduce Pop to her new friends and their husbands. Mom had left everything in California to move to rural Virginia. She was starting over and establishing new relationships from the ground up. Finally, after several months of introductions, Pop looked at her and said, "I already have friends." Harsh sounding? You bet!

Pop was self-aware enough to know that he was at his "Be There" capacity. He was an introvert who needed to have his own time. He valued showing up for his close friends and family and knew his relational limits.

Growing up, I could sense this peace that Pop lived with. He was content with the authentic relationships he had established and hated inauthenticity.

He had his small, tight group of friends from high school, and that's all he could manage. When they needed anything, he was there for them. He despised inauthenticity. He loathed fake small talk and putting up a front to impress anyone.

After Pop passed, one of his close friends told me a story that highlighted how Pop was there for his close friends in meaningful ways. This friend decided to stop drinking alcohol, which was a bold decision in their social circle. Some avoided hanging out with this friend who "didn't want to have fun anymore," but not Pop. Their friendship grew even closer simply because Pop committed to being a constant presence in his friend's life, regardless if he was still in the party scene or not.

The valleys of life help to expose who is really with us. A provider knows what it's like to be in the lowland and can bless others by honoring the person.

When these tough times arise, we need a healthy relationship rather than a toxic addiction to deal with the pain. It's nearly impossible just to conjure these relationships up at the moment. That's why showing up for ourselves and others is such a blessing.

Pop knew he had friends that were like brothers, who would do anything for him, and vice versa. They had proven this to one another over decades. It takes time, so let's start being more present now.

Being present is an active choice we have to make—every single day.

Want to build the skills and confidence it takes to be a provider? Have patience and simply be there for someone. It builds trust, which allows someone to believe and know that you are ready and willing to provide for them.

Take the last days of Pop's life as a case in point of how to *be there* for someone. He invited my brother and me to his house for an intentional conversation just a couple of weeks before his passing. He also showed up at his best friend's house just to see how their building project was progressing. He led my sister in a Bible study, directing her to read a specific chapter for a difficult season in her life. And then he took Mom out to dinner, just the two of them, the night before he died. All of these are examples of *being there*.

Be a provider. Be there.

Be There Challenge: How can you show up for yourself this week? Think of what activity would bring you energy so that you can ultimately bless others. Examples might include reserving uninterrupted time for a hobby, spending money on yourself without feeling guilty, or a simple reflective walk where you ask yourself what you need in this particular season of life to build up your spirit.

BLESSING HABIT #2: BE KNOWN

Hearing Pop's story and seeing how he modeled being known to his two sons will forever be the gold standard of complete vulnerability and willingness to share for the benefit of others. Therefore, *Be Known* earned a spot on the Provider Wheel.

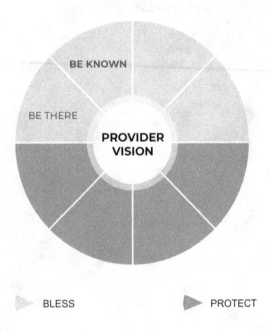

THE PROVIDER WHEEL

Aristotle is often credited with saying that the beginning of all wisdom is knowing ourselves. The surprising truth in this statement is that in order to bless others, we first need to know who we really are.

And knowing ourselves is not necessarily easy! To know thyself and be known by others is an essential element of becoming a provider.

I've had the great pleasure and honor of partaking in men's groups where we shared our life stories in one-hour, uninterrupted slots that were more structured.

I've also experienced being known in 30-second intervals with men as we take a pause to pray at the end of morning workouts. Some of the men have shared intimate details of their lives from suicidal children, job losses, and marital issues.

Whether I am summarizing key moments in my life or sharing what's currently on my heart, this helps me to know myself while being known to others.

The format can change; it just comes down to this question: Are you going to wait for the other person to take the lead on having these conversations, or are you willing to take the lead on going to those vulnerable places?

When we want to have a deeper, more meaningful relationship, we often ask them out. I tried doing this in sixth grade for the first time. I remember channeling all my adolescent strength to call a classmate and ask if she wanted to "go out with me." After she said yes, I had my first girlfriend, but no plan or idea what to do next. I didn't put in any additional effort after that initial ask. Naturally, the relationship did not last. I wasn't ready or willing to be known at this life stage.

Fast forward from middle school to my mid-30s and I was finally ready to be known. It's funny how we can desire to be close to family and friends but never give them permission to make this a reality. I had some ideas of how to improve in this area of my provider journey so I organized a conference call between my brother and my wife. The conversation went something like this:

"John, I want you to know the purpose of doing this is so that I am a better husband, father, and man of God. If at any time you feel like I am missing the mark or not being completely transparent with you, call me out on that. And if that doesn't work, you have my permission to talk with Amy."

I then looked at my wife and spoke back into the phone.

"Amy, if you ever feel like I am not providing for you in Christlike fashion, or you are worried about me being untruthful, you have my permission to ask John anything directly."

I paused and soaked in the moment. It felt like a significant milestone in my relationship with my brother and wife. I was inviting them in. I was trying to add accountability into being known.

To determine our focused topics during our one-on-one time, my brother and I brainstormed four categories:

- Financial Transparency
- Sexual Purity
- Relationship with God
- Family Leadership

Every month we complete a monthly self-assessment in each of the four categories and share it with one another during a phone call. We settled on a Red/Yellow/Green system to keep it simple and honest.

I don't know if Pop ever had this type of conversation with his friends. Still, he did have relationships that lasted decades because he committed to them and knew his relational limits, and I still see the fruits of those relationships to this day.

This focused relationship obviously takes some time and work. It's showing the other person you are showing up but with a specific purpose of being known. After trying this out for myself, my strong encouragement is to do the same! Ask one or two people if they would be willing to go deeper. Try it for three months and have a check-in on the experiment with categories that are important to your personal growth. Another way to think of it is what behaviors need to start, stop, or continue in your life and share that with your friend in a consistent, intentional relationship.

I was also reminded how important it is to not only know others but to know ourselves with an unexpected conversation with the author, speaker, and legend, Mr. Bob Goff.

For those unaware, Bob Goff wrote a fantastic book called *Love Does*. His life story of courage is always a favorite of the men of the fellowship. For those unfamiliar with his work, Bob shares stories from his unorthodox life as a lawyer, diplomat, and nonprofit founder where he builds schools in Africa and beyond. But, believe it or not, this is just the tip of all his incredible life stories. At the end of his book, he gives his personal cell phone number—he probably didn't think his book would turn out to be a *New York Times* bestseller!

I tried calling him right after I finished his book. Unsurprisingly it stated the voicemail was full. A week or so later, I met up with a men's group who had also read the book and asked if anyone else had tried calling Bob. To my surprise, no one had.

We moved on in the conversation and I looked over to see one of the guys motioning us over. He had called Bob in the middle of our discussion, and this time Bob answered! Our conversation was interrupted when Bob Goff went on speakerphone:

"This is Bob."

"Uh . . . hey, Bob," we said, surprised he picked up. We quickly gathered ourselves. "We read your book. It made a real impact on us all."

"Well, you should write a book!" Bob volleyed right back to us. We looked around at one another, surprised.

Bob continued, "If you write a chapter or two about your life now, one day your kids will go running into a burning house to retrieve it. It will mean the most to them of anything you give to them. Go write something about your life, share your story."

And here I am today writing. Thanks, Bob!

I heard this command from Bob before Pop passed. I heard it, but I didn't really grasp what he was saying. I do now. It's worth the time and effort to share our story for the next generation to learn from us, but it starts with having the commitment to know ourselves. We can't share our story until we understand it. Or as the book *Gifts of Imperfection* so beautifully puts it, "I now see how owning our story and loving ourselves through that process is the bravest thing that we will ever do." (Brown, xiv)

The relationships that are so richly formed from being known is why it's worth all the effort. It was a privilege to hear Pop's story from the man himself. After all, there is no one more equipped to share your story than you.

Be a provider. Be known.

Be Known Challenge: Who are you? Try answering this question as if you had to give a 1-hour presentation to a small group of close friends. What would they need to learn about you in order to *really* know who you are? Reflect on the key events, people, and milestones in your journey. The next courageous step would be to actually share this story with someone you trust. Believe me, it will be a blessing for you and them!

BLESSING HABIT #3: BLESSING SPEAKER

The story we tell ourselves impacts our life. Is your self-talk blessing you? Would you say that the majority of thoughts are building you up or tearing yourself down? The power of our words starts with what we are communicating to ourselves. Being a blessing speaker is a critical habit to build into our provider journey.

THE PROVIDER WHEEL

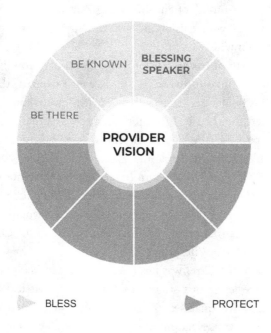

I saw the power of affirmations in my life when I started running.[1] As I got into the practice of running, I found myself being bombarded with an avalanche of negative thoughts from "that last mile was way too slow" to "my legs are not going to make it much longer." Then I made a small, yet dramatic change that made me appreciate the power of speaking blessing in my life.

Whenever I completed a mile, my GPS watch would buzz. I turned off the sound so I was no longer aware of my pace or overall distance. I kept the vibration on to remind me to say the following words of affirmation:

"I'm proud of you, Justin"

I imagine the most important and influential people in my life saying they were proud of me for going one more mile. The joy of running returned with this slight tweak. Our words matter and Pop showed that in my life as well.

He was a man of few words, but when he spoke, you listened. And when he took time to write to you, you treasured those words. Remember his final letter to me? That is worth more than any riches he could have left me. But it wasn't just final remarks that prompted Pop to write or speak blessings into our family. Pop had multiple examples of speaking blessings into his family. He didn't leave things unsaid.

For example, Pop wrote Mom letters during their marriage. Mom remarked how special his writings were because they reflected his true voice. "His letters would be normal things he would say," Mom explained, "things that were authentic and meaningful." One letter he wrote was titled "My Wife."

Pop's "My Wife" letter was not filled with forged Hallmark messages or trendy "love letter tips" found online. In this classic Pop note, he simply wrote down qualities he liked in Mom. He listed out that he respected her caretaker nature and the sound of her voice. He wrote that he thanked God he could find a woman that he could love through the different seasons of life. In this letter, and throughout their marriage, he affirmed her mothering skills. As you might imagine, reflecting on Pop's personal letters has helped us all, and especially Mom, navigate the grieving process.

Pop's letters were not prompted by holidays. In fact, Mom said he hated to be told when to buy presents and would often let holidays pass without doing anything extravagant. This could certainly come across as a cold, insensitive gesture, but he wanted his words and actions to have meaning and not to be forced or disingenuous. A blessing speaker is authentic and deliberate in their words.

Pop also wrote fatherly advice to my sister as she went to college. He took time to deliver it to her in person, and it lists ten proverb-like sayings to help equip her for the next chapter of her life:

God will treat you better than you will treat yourself.
The proof of love is the passion to protect.
Your pain gives birth to your goals;
Your goals choose your mentors;
Your mentors decide your wisdom;
Your wisdom decides your relationships;
Your relationships reveal your self-portrait;
Your self-portrait determines your attitude;
Your attitude decides your access;
Your access decides your favor;
Your favor determines your rewards.

The instructions you follow determines the future *you* create.
Love, Pop.

These are all examples of being a blessing speaker, but what does it really mean?

A blessing speaker is one who intentionally prepares a blessing and speaks it over someone to affirm them. It's thoughtful and prepared. It not only speaks to the person where they are today, but who they will be in the future.

I don't believe we intend to curse anyone. However, that is what we do when we elect not to speak a blessing into their life. We discount the power and responsibility we have to love others the way God wants us.

We think, "When I am a husband, a parent, or just more 'mature,' I will then give a blessing." This is selfish thinking.

Think no one will listen to you? Don't believe this is your calling? Scripture describes this as exactly how Moses acted when God called him to lead the Israelites out of Egypt. You can't keep running away from this opportunity. It's a privilege to speak blessings into someone's life.

During our first fellowship retreat, I encouraged the guys to take an hour to consider who they might deliver a blessing to and begin drafting the letter. I found an empty room, and as the group mentor, I stretched out on the sofa to take a little siesta. However, God had other plans for me during this time.

I immediately sensed that I needed to also participate in the activity I had presented to the men of the fellowship. I went from lying down and trying to take a quick nap, to sitting up and opening up my journal. It didn't take long. I knew who I was to prepare a blessing for.

———

TWO MONTHS LATER

"Mom, we have one more gift to give you."

It was our first Christmas without Pop. The family had all gathered together for our typical family activities, but of course, this holiday was not normal. We had just completed our "Secret Santa" gift exchange, and everyone was seated in the living room. Each year we use a shared Google Doc to update our present suggestions to help our Secret Santa out. It was my painful job that year to remove Pop's name from the spreadsheet. It was just another cruel reminder of his departure.

I cleared my throat. My wife knew what was about to happen, but no one else did. I stood up.

"For our first Christmas together without Pop, I wanted to share some remarks with you. Here is a blessing letter for you and the future of our family." I opened up the letter and began to read it to Mom.

A Blessing for Mom, the Caretaker

A caretaker is one who looks after others. Throughout your life, you have been lovingly caring for those across your journey, from friends and family around the country to those across generational lines. People draw close to you because they know you genuinely care for them. Today, on behalf of all your children, I want to honor and testify how well you have fulfilled the caretaker role in our lives while affirming your purpose now and moving forward.

As your children, we have all experienced your intentional caretaker nature, from investing in our emotional and relational needs growing up to now caring for our very own children. You are always positively active and involved. Your name may change from Mom, Madre, Momma Mia, Ahma, to Ahmee, but you continue to care for others. This calling is still upon your life.

Your commissioned art dream solidifies this truth. You possess grit that perseveres and comes out stronger. You don't give in. You don't give up, especially on people. What if you never gave Pop a second chance to reintroduce himself? We would not be here today.

God has a purpose for this season of your life as the caretaker.

To maximize all the years of caring for others, to now care for yourself. This self-care will allow you to care for others in new and life-changing ways.

How can you receive care now and provide more impact in lives moving forward? God will equip you with the tools to accomplish this in your own unique way. This gift is a representation and reminder of that promise.

Keep praying. Keep showing us God's love. You have more to give to others. And God will provide the ultimate source for that gift.

After I finished reading the blessing to Mom, we presented her with a framed pottery piece that my wife had made. In the blue vase there were flowers. This meant a tremendous amount to Mom. A few months prior, she had shared a vivid dream that represented how she would be able to make it through life without Pop. The dream reminded her that she was strong and capable. This framed vase served as a reminder of that beautiful promise.

It was a special moment, and at the same time, I learned that this process does not need to be perfect.

I stumbled through the delivery of this letter. In fact, I remember skipping a whole line. I hadn't realized how nervous I would be giving it to her. I should have practiced reading it out loud. Fortunately, I gave Mom a copy so she could read the entire letter. It wasn't perfect, and yet it was a success.

This experience also taught me the value of speaking affirmations in my own life. I needed to tell myself that while I made mistakes speaking Mom's blessing, I was loved by her no matter how well I spoke. I was her son; I was trying to become a better provider. There is a reason gratitude journals often have daily affirmations in them—we need them! With all the negative events and voices in our lives, be sure to practice the art of speaking blessing in your own life.

Providing is about embracing the role and opportunity. Just as Pop modeled, it does not need to be a holiday; it just needs to be our authentic observation and positive voice in the life of someone for whom we are called to provide. It could be as simple as a compliment verbalized, not only a written letter. I remember Pop always saying he loved us and that he was proud of us. In order to become a blessing speaker we don't need to use fancy words, just meaningful ones.

Be a provider. Be a blessing speaker.

Blessing Speaker Challenge: How can you incorporate daily words of affirmation in your own life? Using the example of being reminded by the vibrations of the watch during a run, how can you consistently bless yourself with your thoughts and words so you can do the same for others?

BLESSING HABIT #4: BIBLICAL GENEROSITY

Being generous is an admirable goal. We bless ourselves and others when the generosity requires sacrifice that builds up ourselves and others. This is Biblical Generosity.

THE PROVIDER WHEEL

In order to avoid burnout, we have to be willing to be generous to ourselves. Similar to being there, Biblical Generosity prompts us to bless ourselves with generous acts of kindness in order to do the same for others. This is hard. As providers, we want to bless others, to show our generosity, but this has a short shelf life if we aren't first giving to ourselves.

I will never know if Pop would consider himself a generous person. I know without a doubt that he was. And his example of saving and investing in himself highlights how, when we are generous to ourselves, our impact is even greater in the lives of others. I saw this with Pop's career. Because he ran his business wisely and was generous to himself by taking time off when needed and creating a healthy culture in the office, he was able to recognize opportunities to be a blessing to others.

There was the story of the delivery man who worked for Pop, who had lost most of his teeth. This was an hourly employee who would not be working long-term for him, but that didn't matter. One day Pop told the employee to leave work and go over to the dentist. He had scheduled him to get dentures. No charge—Pop covered it for him.

There was also the time Pop and Mom met up at Cracker Barrel for lunch. As they were enjoying their meal together, Mom overheard someone at a nearby table loudly demand to see the manager. Mom watched the dramatic scene unfold as the waitress sobbed and ran off, and the manager appeared. Pop eventually noticed Mom's attention was fixated on the nearby table and asked what was going on. Pop looked towards the table to see the manager walk back into the kitchen, soon seeing the waitress returning with more food and more tears. Pop felt such compassion for the waitress he sprang into action.

"Go give this to her." Pop extended a fifty-dollar bill to Mom. "Tell her tomorrow will be a better day."

"Ok, but why don't you give it to her?" Mom asked.

"Well, it would be awkward for an old man like me to give her money." Mom was impressed with Pop's self-awareness. She hadn't even thought about how the gesture could be viewed as inappropriate. Following his request, Mom walked over to the young waitress and relayed the message to her. This time tears of thanksgiving spread across both of their faces.

Since Pop's passing, I've had the pleasure of hearing more stories like these. Mom summed it up perfectly, "Pop was so generous, he was willing to help someone else make themselves better." Whether it was dentures, a tip, a chainsaw, a job opportunity, or a tuition payment, Pop blessed people through his generosity in practical, meaningful ways.

Pop was also generous beyond money. Some of his most precious gifts to us today are the handmade items that he crafted. Beautiful cutting boards, paintings, and a masterful rocking horse that our daughters enjoy are just some of the examples of how he was generous with his time and talents.

It's simply amazing what happens when we invest in ourselves and how much stronger the ripple effects are for others. When we are grounded in Biblical generosity, we are not investing in ourselves for our own gain, rather we are enjoying and using the gifts God has given us for the benefit of others.

God was smiling down on Pop when he dedicated all those hours in his basement workshop to master his woodworking skills, because Pop used his expertise to bless his family with an heirloom gift to his grand-daughters.

Be a provider. Be Biblically generous.[2]

Biblical Generosity Challenge: How can you be generous to your-self this week? What considerate act can you do for yourself that blesses you? Consider not only one-time events like a purchase for yourself, but habits that can be done weekly or daily. This will equip you to then bless others with your generosity.

———————————— CHAPTER SUMMARY ————————————

KEY TAKEAWAYS

- **Being there is the starting point:** Our physical presence can be a gift to ourselves and others. Don't discount this blessing opportunity.

- **Being known can be accomplished in short bursts or longer events:** It's not the *time* that allows us to be known, it's whether or not we are willing to be authentic and vulnerable.
- **Our words matter:** Scripture describes how our words can either speak blessings or curses in our life and to others.
- **Generosity starts with ourselves and then ripples to others.** By caring for ourselves, we are then able to recognize how to bless others with sacrifices that are sustainable while using our unique gifts.

CHALLENGE

Choose one of the four blessing habit challenges presented in this chapter and try the one that most resonates with you.

---

1. Capturing affirmations using a journal such as the 5 Minute Journal also helped develop this habit https://www.intelligentchange.com/products/the-five-minute-journal
2. If you want to take a deeper dive in exploring Jesus-like generosity I highly recommend the non-profit Generous Giving at https://generousgiving.org/

CHAPTER 9

The Protecting Habits

So far, the Provider Wheel has offered some intentional blessing activities and habits that can be a lot of fun. From showing up and being generous to sharing encouragement with close friends, these are some of life's memorable moments! Now we get to the bottom of the Provider Wheel. These are the protection habits in our lives that others may not see, yet are an equal part in the provider journey.

PROTECTING HABIT #1: PREPARED

While the protecting habits may initially go unnoticed, they are critical when the moment demands, particularly our first habit of *Being Prepared.*

THE PROVIDER WHEEL

Preparing ourselves for the day is a great micro-case study in the first protecting habit. These small decisions can have a lasting difference in the quality of our day. I immediately think of Admiral William McRaven's commencement speech to drive home this point of how seemingly mundane acts of preparedness can positively influence our entire day:

> "If you make your bed every morning you will have accomplished the first task of the day. It will give you a small sense of pride, and it will encourage you to do another task and another and another. By the end of the day, that one task completed will have turned into many tasks completed. Making your bed will also reinforce the fact that little things in life matter. If you can't do the little things right, you will never do the big things right." (McRaven)

When we control what we can control, we are practicing the skill of being prepared. We never know when our day will go in unexpected ways, and protecting ourselves with intentional actions will help us develop the confidence to handle the surprises.

———

"Stay in the store. No one comes out," Pop calmly instructed everyone in the furniture store. He firmly placed the office phone back on the desk, and Mom could sense this was a profound moment.

"A customer just called and said he was on his way to the store. I'm going to go outside to meet him." There was a pause before he continued, "He threatened to kill me," and then he repeated his initial instructions, "Everyone stays inside."

Pop then went to the large steel and concrete office safe. His hands were deliberate and steady as he spun the lock to enter the combination code. Mom's eyes were white with fear. She had just arrived at the family furniture store to visit Pop. It was common for her to help decorate the store's window display and keep the furniture store feeling like an extension of the home. However, this was no longer a routine office visit.

Mom watched Pop draw out his handgun from the safe. It was the first time she was watching him drawing his gun out for self-defense.

He was ready for the moment. Then, without saying another word, he walked out the front door and locked it behind him.

Mom waited. The minutes seemed like an eternity.

"God, please protect him," Mom kept praying over and over as she waited.

A soft bell rang, the one hanging on the front door indicating someone was entering the store. Mom stood up and ran to the front. It was Pop. He was the definition of calm, cool, and collected, walking back to the office as if nothing major had happened.

"I'm fine. We agreed he could pay his bills at a later time." Pop then went back to the safe and safely returned his gun. No shots were needed, and no one was hurt. Pop acted as the mailman had just casually delivered a standard package, and he was going about his day as usual. This was far from reality, however. A customer had become so angry over a billing issue that he threatened to kill Pop and came to the store in a rage. Remember, this is rural Southwest Virginia, a small town of just a couple thousand blue-collar workers.

Pop never seemed to be rattled by a situation. He was always prepared and addressed issues head-on. Can you imagine that happening to you? This isn't about arming yourself or protecting the Second Amendment. This story demonstrates how prepared Pop lived his life (and shows he was a modern-day John Wayne figure).

I'm sure Pop didn't expect an angry customer to threaten his life that day when he arrived at the store that morning. But he was ready. As Mom put it, "He was totally Mr. Prepared." Pop always carried a pocket knife and cash on him. He always would have a cooler with drinks in his car and in the trunk, a winter coat, extra quarts of oil, and tools. He would rarely let his gas tank fall below half a tank.

Pop embodied being prepared. During the fellowship, we talk about denying ourselves today so that we can be prepared for tomorrow. That is what being prepared is all about, sacrificing immediate comfort for future gain.

Being prepared spans across a variety of facets of our lives. More times than not, we are living life in a rush with a busy schedule. It's hard to think ahead. We may even justify rushing to our next appointment and skipping the gas station just one more time, even though the empty light is flashing red. The perceived benefit of driving outweighs the risk of not filling up. We are often too busy to stop for gas when our life is barely running on fumes.

The tension between addressing the here and now versus preparing for future needs clash again and again. A leader who matters is ready for the challenges of the day because they have been diligent and put on the armor, ready for the inevitable flaming arrows of life.

I've had many occasions of *not* being prepared in life.

—————

"Let's take a picture before you leave with the backpack," my wife called out to me.

"It's a rucksack," I playfully corrected her, smiling.

I was just minutes away from leaving to go to my fifth GoRuck endurance challenge and was feeling confident. After months of training, I was about to leave for the start of the event. I was all smiles until I noticed my bag was damp. After investigating, I realized my water bladder was leaking. Apparently, during one of my final training sessions, it had been punctured. Not good!

I had gone from confidence to chaos. I had felt fully prepared just a second ago, and now I felt like a novice, totally unprepared. I had to have a functioning three-liter water bladder for the event. It was a requirement to participate, and the event was just a couple of hours from commencing.

What to do? Duct-tape it? Run out to the store? I was going through my options, and none sounded good. I needed to be confident it would hold up during the challenge, and who knew what kind of weight pressure it would be under during the event, so duct tape wouldn't work. And I really didn't want to go to a Wal-Mart or big box store out of the way and risk being late—that would have severe consequences, not only for me but the entire team!

Then I remembered my neighbor, Gail. He and I had done some training together leading up to the event. He hadn't even signed up for this particular event but supported me in the build-up to the challenge. I called him up.

"What's up, Justin, you ready for the big night?"

"Hey man," I said as I quickly got to business. "My water bladder broke and I need a replacement. Do you have anything I could use… like right now?" I paused.

"Of course, come on over, use whatever you need!"

I quickly left, bypassing the pre-event picture, and raced over to my friend's house. Not only did I get a replacement water source, but he upgraded some of my other equipment for the event. Wow! I had gone from the valley to the mountain of emotions in just a few minutes. I was now even *more* prepared for the challenge. I had put in the work, but that wasn't enough; I needed the help of a friend at the last minute to help me overcome an unexpected challenge. I smiled as I drove to the challenge, much more thankful for my upgraded equipment and for my friend.

The purpose of *being prepared* isn't always to have the equipment, but rather the relationships to help you overcome challenges that you haven't had time or foresight to prepare for.

Be prepared. Be a provider.

Prepared Challenge: Prepare for the day by simply making your bed. While this may seem an odd way to prepare, it helps to remind us of what we can control and to construct our day with intentionality.

PROTECTING HABIT #2: PHYSICAL FITNESS

A provider puts in the hard work, including caring for his or her body. It's absolutely critical to have the energy and stamina to do the work necessary in life.

THE PROVIDER WHEEL

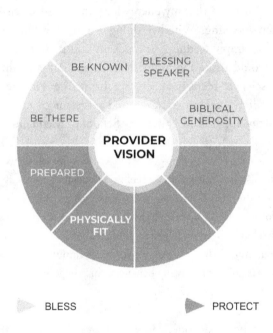

I've mentioned the word "energy" several times in this book and let's take a moment to dive into this feeling. Another way of describing the sensation of having energy is feeling enthusiastic. Imagine a life where you are living fully charged up and experiencing activities that you enthusiastically look forward to enjoying. This is a life full of energy. So how do we get to experience that? You may assume diet and exercise, but I would propose that it begins with having curiosity around your physical fitness.

Be genuinely curious about your body. When do you feel energized during the day and document what triggers that level of enthusiasm. Be sure to also capture the moments where you feel depleted. It's important to become aware of what serves us and what drains us. While there are some universal truths around healthy living, the provider journey requires us to invest in identifying our specific health triggers.

For me, I realized that my energy level improved when I spent time outside each morning. Whether doing a morning workout with the men of F3 or simply feeding our chickens and pigs at our mini-homestead, this would make me more alert for the day and this is actually backed by science. Here is an excerpt from The Tim Ferriss podcast with Dr. Andrew Huberman, a tenured professor of neurobiology and ophthalmology at Stanford University School of Medicine:

> "Our visual system is perhaps the strongest lever by which we can shift our state of mind and body . . . biology is encouraging us, if you will, to take on the right behaviors, which are to get outside. Even if there's cloud cover, there's a lot more light energy, a lot more photons coming through cloud cover than you're going to get off your phone or a computer. And early in the day, two to 10 minutes outside without sunglasses is going to be really beneficial for a huge range of biological functions and brain state." (Huberman)

Pop loved being outside. He would work all day at the furniture store, come home, and then change out of his professional clothes and get into his preferred uniform of white t-shirt and faded jeans.

Whenever Pop was inside, he never seemed comfortable. The man who sold furniture for a living preferred to sit on an end table during the brief moments he took a break to watch tv or sit with the family. Pop always seemed more at ease in motion. He would get on the tractor to mow and then spread more gravel down our nearly two-mile-long driveway. He would then spend time in the garden tilling up the ground to reap a harvest later in the growing season. Another evening he might use the chainsaw to clean up broken trees on our driveway from a storm and then stack the freshly cut wood on our front porch to have it ready for the wood-burning stove. There was a lot to maintaining our home in the mountains of rural Virginia that I never truly appreciated.

My brother teared up as he reflected about Pop the week of his passing. "He was the hardest worker I ever saw. I want to be like that." The work that my brother and I both witnessed was more than just office work. In fact, to us, *work* was what he did around the house we grew up in.

Pop knew his responsibilities and worked hard to fulfill those responsibilities. This was how he exercised. There was never a gym membership or formal training routine. He kept himself strong in order to complete the activities required for our household.

Being *physically fit* not only allows us to fulfill our chores, but it is also a provider habit that enables us to protect others. Think back to the image of a shepherd guarding and comforting his sheep in Psalm 23. It's hard to feel comfortable unless you feel safe. I always felt safe around Pop.

Being a safe and strong provider goes beyond the strength to physically protect your family or friend in a fight. That moment may come occasionally, but what is guaranteed are our daily, mundane physical needs. We tend not to appreciate how fortunate most of us are to have healthy bodies capable of blessing and protecting those in our life. Whether it's chopping wood or simply changing a light, this requires us to be active and not on the couch.

I'm reminded of one of my hikes in middle school. A few friends and I ventured out, and we ended up getting lost. When night fell, we decided we better not continue and settled into a camping site and built a fire while waiting for help. This was before everyone had cell phones, so we were lost in the woods with no forms of communication.

My friends' parents reported us lost to the park rangers who started the search party that night. What did Pop do when he heard the news? He loaded up his horse and trailer and drove an hour to help join the search party! He didn't ask for permission; he went into action, and he was physically ready for the task. The park rangers located us first, but I will never forget seeing Pop on the horse as we walked back to the trailhead. Like many of these provider habits, you may not know when or how you will use them, but they will be called upon as you bless and protect others when they are lost in life.

This provider characteristic of health is fundamental to me as a health coach and executive of a health and wellness company. As a provider, it's all about blessing and protecting others while also maintaining our core strength to ensure we have something to give. So let's not discount our health anymore.

It's plain and simple. We have one body. It's not even really ours. We were given this by God and we have the opportunity to honor Him through our bodies. And we haven't even talked about the great side effects of being *physically fit* with more productive work and mental clarity.

As an integrative health coach, I have learned that health and wellness are about much more than food and exercise. Similarly, the Provider Wheel offers a holistic picture of habits and traits to be a healthy provider.

Be a provider. Be physically fit.

Physically Fit Challenge: List out 3-5 activities that are physically active and bring you energy. Consider activities that you would enthusiastically do, then you'll know you are on the right track of protecting yourself in authentic ways! Think creatively such as gardening, disc golf, jumping on the trampoline with the kids, hiking, etc. Prioritize at least one of your preferred activities this week so that you have the energy to protect not only yourself but others.

PROTECTING HABIT #3: PERSONAL INTEGRITY

Character and integrity also earned a spot on the Provider Wheel because we must consistently live out high moral standards to have the honor of providing for others.

THE PROVIDER WHEEL

We all have to live with ourselves. Friends may come and go, we transition jobs and careers, yet there is no replacing that person in the mirror. We have to live with the decision we make.

I'll never forget a painful moment during my MBA program where I was disappointed in myself. I tried going to bed but couldn't stop thinking about how I had engaged in a level of backstabbing and improper behavior that weighed heavy on my mind.

My study team was having internal strife and two of our members were at one another's throats as we prepared our final presentation. The stress of the program had mounted and the cracks were showing. My disgruntled teammates each came to me privately, complaining and gossiping in frustration about the other one. I'm ashamed to say I played both sides.

My integrity was non-existence. I told myself I was offering sympathy but in reality my integrity was non-existent when I fell into the trap of appeasement. I wasn't willing to act bravely . . . at least at first. I literally couldn't sleep with myself, and after a restless night, I called a team meeting. I admitted my role in the implosion of our team and asked us to forgive and move forward. I'll never forget my teammate then extending his hand to me and the other insulted party to show how he was ready and willing to move on.

And that night I slept much better!

Personal integrity takes courage. Some of us have a default personality to speak directly, but we can all develop this skill.

———

"Hey Pop, come over here." I motioned for him to come over to the desk. It was Christmas and the whole family was spending time together at the Lodge. Little did anyone realize that this would turn out to be Pop's last Christmas with us.

"I just had my team at work take this online personality test." I started selling him on the process because I really didn't think that he would actually take the time to sit down at the computer and take a silly online quiz. But I tried anyway and continued my sales pitch, "It will only take a few minutes, and we've all done it. Want to give it a shot?"

"Ha, OK, what do I do?" Pop grinned.

"Just read and select the option that feels most authentic. Let me know when you are done."

To my pleasant surprise, Pop sat down and started taking the online test. I gave him space, and about ten minutes later, he motioned me back over. The results would help me understand and appreciate him in new ways and unlock another key provider habit.

"Well, what does it say?" Pop asked.

Now the whole family's attention was on me as everyone stopped what they were doing in the living room and looked over at the computer desk. We knew Pop was a unique man with clear strengths and weaknesses, yet we were still intrigued to learn more. It would be interesting to see what an online survey would highlight. I read the summary notes out loud:

> "If you are going to get something done, you do it, meeting your obligations no matter what the personal cost, and you are baffled by people who don't hold their own word in the same respect. Combining laziness and dishonesty is the quickest way to get on your bad side."

The family busted out laughing with that final line. Pop was known to say that he "hated a liar and a thief." We heard him say it regularly and this survey result pinpointing laziness and dishonesty as despised character traits was spot on! Even Pop was laughing hard, the type of belly laugh that produces tears in the eyes.

Looking back on this test, the results were really highlighting the characteristic trait of being a person of integrity, someone who gets the job done and is responsible for their actions. Being honest and direct when necessary to ensure the goal is accomplished.

Personal integrity includes being willing to speak the truth. Pop was never afraid to tell the truth, to tell it like it was. Ambiguity frustrated him. He was not scared to talk directly to people, whether it was with customers, friends, or family. Growing up in this environment could be difficult, but it was a wonderful gift to have a father speak the truth.

These types of individuals are willing to protect you from your blind spots and help you grow and do not shy away from the moment.

Personal integrity is also displayed through honoring our word.

Mom has told me countless stories of how much she respected Pop's character of doing what he said he would do. When Pop told Mom that he would take care of something, she believed him, whether it was providing financially or fixing things around the house. In fact, during his final days, Mom told Pop of a loose step on the walkway up to the house. He was mixing mortar in a bucket the next day, and not only did he fix the step that Mom pointed out, but he also identified several other loose ones. All of this just days before suffering a fatal heart attack. This is what having integrity does; it can help protect others when they have shaky foundations because the provider's character is strong. I smile every time I walk up those steps. The mortar is slightly darker and stands out among the rest. *Personal integrity* will help you stand out to others in a positive way.

Pop had no problem looking people in the eye, telling them they disappointed him and that something was unacceptable. I had some friends who worked at Pop's furniture store with me during our high school days. My friend Matt reflected on this time with his own authentic and direct style: "Justin, your dad did not mince his words. He could verbally undress you, but at the same time, I always knew he was doing it to make me better and that he cared." That is a provider.

One recent example of developing *personal integrity* to be a better provider was after a storm came through our neighborhood. The following day, I looked out in our backyard and saw a big cedar tree had damaged limbs with thick branches laying on the ground and more that needed to come down. My wife remarked how we would need to get someone to come out and take it away. I said I would take care of it. Then, nodding skeptically, she went back to her morning coffee.

I'm not sure what happened. Perhaps Pop's death had inspired me, knowing he would own up to this need and get it down. I finished up my work early that same day, bought a new chainsaw, and took it down that evening. Fortunately, I did not lose any limbs! It was the quickest turnaround I could have possibly done. We had a half-fallen tree, and now it was entirely down and no longer a risk to our girls as they played in the backyard. It was a proud moment for me. I had lived out *personal integrity*, but it's a habit that demands our ongoing attention.

Having integrity means we accept responsibility when we have failed, acknowledge our weakness, and commit to building a stronger foundation—especially when no one is around. Taking ownership and doing what we say we are going to do is the place to start developing this provider habit.

Be a provider. Have personal integrity.

Personal Integrity Challenge: Reflect on a time when you were disappointed in yourself. Use that shame for good. Recall how you never want to compromise in that way again and put up boundaries in your life to protect yourself while you build back up your integrity. Whether that is sharing a weakness of your life with a close friend or a certified therapist, think about ways of building back up this area so you can protect yourself and stop limiting the positive influence you can have in the lives of others.

PROTECTING HABIT #4: PRAYERFUL

Believing in something greater than ourselves helps us become better providers. Having the humility that we need to be protected in our lives opens the door for having a rich, prayerful life.

THE PROVIDER WHEEL

There are volumes of books written on prayer and I don't want to pretend to be an expert here. You may be like me with an ever-changing commitment level to prayer. There can be a lot of inappropriate baggage on what you should say, how to pray, etc. Let's strip all that away and remember that prayer protects us from ourselves by reminding us that we need help and enables us to form a true relationship with God. I believe we can find true delight in a "real friendship with God as compared with occasional feelings of His presence in prayer." (Chambers, 80)

So how can we use prayer in our provider journey? Pop modeled to me a way to make prayer more "sticky," ways to take verses that stood out along his spiritual journey and use it to create a heartfelt, custom prayer.

Mom was preparing for the day. She heard Pop's familiar voice outside the bedroom in the kitchen. It was early, and a regular ritual was happening. Pop was starting the day out by reading the Scriptures out loud. A few minutes later, Pop came into the room and started getting ready for the day in the bathroom, this time reciting his daily prayer out loud. Mom sipped her coffee and felt comforted. It was a daily habit, Pop verbally reciting his memorized prayers.

On the day of Pop's funeral reception, we had a family-only morning brunch. The idea was to give us a moment as a family to gather before hosting and seeing friends. I wasn't sure how the event would go. It's an awkward event to lead. You want to be friendly and authentic as you grieve while giving people direction and let them know it's OK not to be OK. I brought Pop's Bible with me and welcomed everyone.

Our extended family of around forty people huddled around my aunt and uncle's living room. I tried to make them feel less uneasy. I stated that although it was a time of loss, this was also a time to be comforted and encouraged. I shared how Pop recited a prayer each morning from his Bible and that I wanted to read it aloud. I reached down and picked up Pop's Bible.

Pop's Bible is older than I am. It is bound with aged black leather that has now dried and cracked. The back is literally duct-taped together. If that doesn't speak to a man's character having a well-worn Bible, I don't know what else does! Earlier I shared how Pop had a handwritten prayer on the inside of the front cover. Here it is in its entirety:

> *I am the body of Christ, and Satan has no power over me, I overcome evil with good for the greater one dwells within me. I fear no evil for Thou art with me, Your Word and Your Spirit, they comfort me. I am far from oppression and fear does not overcome me. No weapons formed against me will prosper, but everything I do will prosper. I am delivered from the evils of this present world, and I am redeemed from the curse of the Law. I refuse to receive any sickness or disease to come upon this body, for it is God's will. He has given His angels charge over me to keep me in all my ways, in my pathway of life, there is no death. I am a doer of the Word of God. In the name of Jesus, Amen.*

After reading out loud to my extended family, there was a quiet peace in the room. I was impressed and comforted that Pop had this powerful life prayer. It was a special moment for the entire family to peer into Pop's private prayer time ritual. Here was a very practical example of how prayer blesses and protects. We were a grieving family, one trying to grapple with an unexpected loss. Pop's prayer was like a healing ointment to our fresh wound. It didn't make the pain go away, yet it started the recovery process. He had pulled together Scripture that spoke to him and made it part of his daily routine.

Mom then shared how comforting it was to witness Pop's prayer muscle the moment his body's strength left him. He was praying during his last moments, his hands outstretched. What will our final words be? If we develop a prayerful habit like Pop, perhaps we, too, can experience our version of a last peaceful moment.

As Oswald Chambers once reflected, "To say that 'prayer changes things' is not as close to the truth as saying, 'Prayer changes me and then I change things.'" (Chambers 501)

We need to get to know God through prayer, receive His guidance, and use the blessings and protection we receive to *change things for others*. The protection we receive is the Lord Himself through prayer who helps us change into the provider we are capable of becoming.

Be a provider. Be a prayerful person.

Prayerful Challenge: Create your own daily prayer. Reference scriptures that inspire you and remind you that you are not the ultimate provider. When we have an authentic prayer life, we have a more personal relationship with God, the one who ultimately provides for us and others.

So there you have it! The full Provider Wheel. Before you proceed with the chapter summary on the protection habits, I want you to take a pause. You have just taken a deeper dive into what may be all new habits that feel overwhelming to introduce in your daily life.

I want to encourage you to give each area of the Provider Wheel equal importance, but to focus on one habit at a time. Remember, these eight habits should bless and protect you first and foremost so you avoid burn-out and only then can you enjoy new levels of energy and stamina to provide for others. I hope this message inspires you and frees you up to start investing in yourself in new, meaningful ways that ultimately increases your fuel capacity to love others even more than you are able to currently.

---————————— **CHAPTER SUMMARY** ——————————

KEY TAKEAWAYS

- **Be ready for the unexpected**: Life will throw us many curveballs, so it is up to us to prepare the best we can to handle them appropriately.
- **Let's not discount our health anymore**: We have one body and it's not even really ours. We were given this body by God and we have the opportunity to honor Him through our physical fitness.
- **Integrity is taking ownership and doing what we say we are going to do**: Honoring our word helps us to trust ourselves and build rapport with others to become a better protector. This habit also allows us to be the same person in every situation, bravely standing up for others when things go wrong.
- **Prayer demonstrates humility**: Relying on God, the ultimate provider for our protection and guidance in life requires us to swallow our pride and ask for help through prayer.

CHALLENGE

Choose one of the four protecting habit challenges presented in this chapter and try the one that most resonates with you.

CHAPTER 10

Turn Your Story Around

You may be thinking your history precludes you from becoming the ideal provider figure described in the previous chapters. Allow me to blow that lie up with a grenade by sharing Pop's past.

———

"Feel free to ask me any questions. It may help me remember more," Pop began. John and I sat at the kitchen counter, silent as Pop started to share his story. Over the next several hours, Pop shared more weaknesses and failures in his life than I had ever dreamed existed. I was on the edge of my seat in disbelief. Pop lived up to his initial description of "exposing himself." He genuinely wanted to be known and understood by his sons.

After he had shared what was on his heart, Pop suggested we go to dinner. It was here that we took our final picture together that now hangs in my office. John and I were about to leave for the night to return to our wives, but I needed to ask Pop a final question.

"How much of this story can I share?"

Pop's eyes shined and a boyish smile lit up his face before responding.

"Well, you can share what you wish. I didn't want this public when you kids were growing up, but if you think it will help and they will want to know, I'll let you make that decision."

Thank you, Pop (and Mom), for giving me permission to share how Pop turned his story around and how we can all do the same.

FROM PASSIVENESS TO PROVIDER

Pop was the prodigal son in many ways. While his father was a respected businessman in town, the twenty-four year old Pop was floundering to find his footing as a young man. So his father invited Pop to start working at the family furniture business, which he begrudgingly accepted.

Around this time, the draft came out for the Vietnam War. Pop received a deferment for his hearing impairment and worked at the family furniture store. Life was starting to become predictable and unfulfilling for Pop. It was time for a decision on how he would use his time and skills in life. One of Pop's friends at the time described Pop as sharp and not afraid to step across the line. "If he had gotten the credentials, he could have worked in the CIA, I'm sure of it," he said. Instead of the CIA, Pop chose to enjoy the party scene.

While Pop had stable employment and the beginnings of establishing a comfortable life, he was a restless soul. He would go on long road trips in the summer and still enjoyed hanging out with his high school friends who mostly stayed in the area. After high school, Pop moved into a house with five other guys. It was an old building with just three bedrooms. It was set up with a bar and kegs of beer. One of Pop's friends later described the parties as including "motorcycles and hotrods, shooting guns, and running kind of wild."

Five sounds like a large enough tenant roster, but many more friends were likely to be spotted on the sofa or floor on any given night. It was *the* hangout location in town. One of Pop's high school friends had moved away and stayed at the house nearly every weekend—even though he lived and worked all the way in Boston!

Pop described this community as a brotherhood, one that he would rely on through good times and bad. He laughed, describing how they were never short on women or motorcycles during these days. I was imagining him living out the movie *Animal House*.

Their reputation in the small town was "Club Mac" when one of their fathers remarked, "This place always has people coming and going; it's like a 24/7 McDonald's."

Things started to get out of hand when marijuana was introduced in Club Mac. The guys started to go to parties in nearby towns to get their pot stash, and Pop recognized an opportunity.

Instead of imitating his father selling used cars on the side for extra cash, Pop started using his business skills on the other side of the law as a small-time drug dealer. At first, he just wanted to make sure he had some for his house parties. But, as he searched for meaning and pleasure, he discovered drugs and the lucrative business of selling marijuana. That's right—Pop, my father and model provider figure, was a drug dealer.

Pop quickly learned that he could earn much more money selling drugs than furniture and started selling marijuana for quick cash. Keep in mind, this was the 1970s before medical marijuana was embraced. In fact, it had just been outlawed with the Controlled Substance Act. Although he lived in a small town, this quickly developed beyond a small-time operation. Pop organized substantial drug deals in Southwest Virginia. He enjoyed the freedom that came from having extra money and the thrill of living on the edge.

What started out as small purchases for his house parties escalated quickly. "He only had high-quality stuff," remarked one of his friends. Pop's desire for travel and freedom paired well for growing his drug business. According to another friend, "Pop was living pretty large— spending money and all, it was a pretty substantial operation. Not just buying and selling pot; this was an enterprise."

Eventually, Pop was making some cross-country trips from Virginia to Arizona to get a trunk full of marijuana that was shipped in from Mexico. He would then transport the product back himself. In fact, one time Pop stopped on the side of Route 66 to take his dog out for a walk, and a cop pulled up behind him. He kept his cool, and when the officer asked if everything was all right, he pointed to the dog and calmly said yes—though his heart was racing, knowing what was in the trunk. Although safe this time, the drug runs eventually caught the attention of the FBI.

The FBI's Drug Enforcement Agency (the DEA) had just been created in 1973, and they had received the backing of the president, himself, to prosecute and convict drug dealers harshly.

This did not deter the young prodigal son.

Eventually, Pop's trunk-load deliveries escalated to tractor-trailer loads of drugs, and inevitably, his name was brought up to the authorities. Some assume it was his drug-dealing partner, and others believe an undercover cop discovered Pop's side hustle. What is certain is that there was a federal warrant out for Pop's arrest. Jail time was expected to be around five years for illegally purchasing and distributing marijuana across state lines.

When Pop heard that his name had been turned into the authorities, he had a decision to make.

Face the reality of his actions and take responsibility or . . . not.

Pop chose to run. One day he was at the furniture store and the next no one heard from him. It was the beginning of a dark period in his life. Pop was officially on the run and off the grid starting in 1974.

For nearly five years, he was a fugitive on the run.

Pop went from living the high life, counting his next six-figure deal one moment in Arizona, to thinking about the reality of jail time. Timing was not on Pop's side as the newly formed DEA had just been created and President Nixon had declared an all-out war against the sale and usage of illegal drugs.

Pop wanted to avoid jail time for him and his prized possession—a Harley Davidson motorcycle. He had a Harley Chopper, one that was straight out of the 1969 Peter Fonda cult classic, *Easy Rider.* Pop's bike was custom-built, loud, and leaked a lot of oil. It was part of Pop's identity. Similar to the movie, Pop was about to start his spiritual journey.

However, unlike the movie, he would not be driving his motorcycle as part of the escape. It was tagged and too easy to spot. He put it in storage in Arizona and mailed the key back to some of his Club Mac roommates.

Back in Radford, Virginia, the Club Mac brothers heard the news. They knew Pop was dealing drugs, but this was a shock. An FBI arrest warrant? It all sounded so surreal and serious, especially in their small town. They all assumed their phones were tapped and did not try to make contact with their friend to protect him.

One of Pop's friends did receive contact through the letter that included a key to a storage unit and instructions on how to retrieve and hide his Harley. The friend recruited another Club Mac member by saying, "I have a mission from CL."

The two of them ended up driving straight to Tucson, Arizona, with no stops other than gas fill-ups. They loaded up the bike on a trailer and drove back just as fast, taking the tags off and hiding it, hoping to see their friend again.

Pop had made his decision. He had to cut all ties and leave everyone and everything he knew. Without a word, the prodigal son was gone. He had run away from his problems. He also assumed the feds were following his friends back in Virginia and tracking their phone conversations. He was alone but felt like he had all he needed, some cash and his two trusty Doberman dogs.

Pop was officially on the run.

The FBI sprang into action. They knew Pop's name, address, work, family, and close friends. The chase was on.

Pop's parents heard about the warrant but did not talk about it much to their other two children. They didn't want to jeopardize their children in any way. They knew the high stakes involved. Therefore, Pop's siblings were in the dark as to his whereabouts and even regarding the extent of his crimes. Pop had always been the wild one in the family, and if someone was going to jail, it was not surprising that their youngest brother was on the verge of doing serious time. This was a stressful time for the Thomas family. Pop's parents were doing what they thought best by proceeding with life and trying to protect their family.

Pop's sister, Nancy, was at home with her twin babies one day when a heavy knock interrupted a peaceful morning playtime. Two federal agents were at the door. "Are you CL Thomas's sister?" one asked Nancy. She nodded yes.

Nancy stood at the door with her two young girls as one agent asked questions and the other read her body language without saying a word the entire time. The assumption was that Pop's family knew where he was or may have been hiding his drug stash or cash. The reality was Pop was long gone and removed from his family. He had not communicated with family since the arrest warrant. His sister was only left with the consistent response, "I don't know."

The agents left that day but kept tracking not only Nancy, but also their brother, Joe. However, neither sibling knew where their younger brother was or what he was up to at that moment. Pop's father told the authorities that he was not supporting his son on the run and would encourage him to turn himself in if he heard from him. As the days turned into weeks without any word from him, Pop's mother started saving twenty-dollar bills around the house for her lost son. When he surfaced, she would be ready. Unfortunately, the pain and sense of hopelessness only intensified for Pop's mom during this time.

Federal agents went as far west as Arizona and north into Canada searching for him. They wanted to make a statement that drug-dealing across state lines was a felony. Meanwhile, Pop kept dodging the authorities as he bounced around Virginia, Tennessee, North Carolina, and even down to Mexico, and eventually settled on a ranch in California. He took on aliases, trusting no one during this time. He would tell acquaintances he met on the run that he was going north, and then head south. He needed to stay one step ahead of the authorities.

There were some close calls during his time on the run. One time a police helicopter located Pop's whereabouts in Arizona and searched up and down with a spotlight in the middle of the night. Another time Pop heard a *click* on his landline phone and knew it was bugged. He quickly ran out of the house, leaving a burning fire in the fireplace to escape the oncoming cops.

I had always assumed Pop had lived a stereotypical life of working, having kids, and providing financially. Now I was grappling with how much he had changed through serious challenges and poor decisions before becoming that model provider.

It was not all fun and adventures on the run. There were times of loneliness and uncertainty to push through. Then, there was a tragic loss.

While Pop was still on the run, his mother died of cancer.

Because Pop accepted what was happening to him as a fugitive, he elected not to provide for anyone else during this time. He would later feel the pain of not being able to attend his mother's funeral. His mom was left wondering, "Where is my son?" on her deathbed.

Fortunately, God was blessing and protecting Pop during this time.

He headed west until he got just about as far from his home state of Virginia. He landed in Northern California, in a small town called Grass Valley. He was sitting in a local bar and knew it was the right town for him when another customer rode their horse through the front door and placed their order, and then the animal took a huge dump on the floor, to the dismay of the bartender.

Pop ended up getting hired as a farmhand with a small, private residence on the property so he could serve as the watchman and protect the property and animals. This point of the story really hit home, because I was realizing this is how Pop met Mom. He was on the run when he met Mom . . . so I had to ask the question when hearing this story for the first time.

"Hey Pop, what name did you meet Mom under?" I asked.

"Well, under the alias of Ken Cheney."

The knowledge that Mom met Pop, not by his real name, but under a different identity, was even bigger news than that he was a drug dealer on the run from the FBI! How could Mom ever marry a guy who was operating with a false identity? She met Pop as the prodigal son, before I knew him as Pop the provider. It's easy for me to write this book when

I know the man Pop became; it's much more impressive that Mom saw the provider traits in Pop during those years on the run.

The two immediately connected at a party. Pop was the mysterious cowboy with thinning hair, a bold beard and a quiet confidence. Even though Pop was living out of his van with his dogs, looking for work, Mom was drawn to him and the two quickly started dating. They went out to the movies and eventually Pop found work as a ranch hand at a nearby horse farm.

Keep in mind Pop and Mom had no business being together. Here he was on the run across the country with no long-term plan and no chance at a long-term relationship with a woman he was lying to everyday.

Ironically enough, Pop was starting to attend a church at this time. His soul was trying to reconcile his desire to start a new life with the harsh realities of his current situation. His newfound passion for reading the Bible resulted in him sharing his favorite Proverbs with everyone he was around—all while lying to Mom about his identity and concealing his past mistakes.

During one visit to the farm, Mom brought Pop's mail to him that he had been forwarding to her address. One handwritten letter with a new name on the return address stood out to Mom.

"Who is Herman Thomas?" Mom asked Pop as she handed him the letter. "That's my father's name," Pop calmly replied, but offered no explanation. In the moment, Mom thought perhaps he was adopted and let the conversation fade off. It would later prove to be a sign of things to come.

After nearly five years on the run, the FBI went on to bigger drug dealers and Pop had settled into life on a horse farm without much noise from the outside, enjoying his new relationships, but his conscience was beginning to awaken. After receiving news that his mother had died and meeting the girl who he knew could be "the one," Pop decided it was time to change. It was time to turn his life around, which meant turning himself in. He contacted his pastor in California and his father back home in Virginia to strategize.

The pastor later recalled Pop asking to speak with him in private the first time they met at a Bible study in California. Pop confided his true identity and desire to make things right by ending his time on the run. Both the pastor and his father supported Pop's decision. It was time to face his past.

The pastor offered to go with Pop when he turned himself in, and he suggested they travel to San Diego because it had a more lenient attitude towards drug charges compared to Northern California's harsher prisons.

Before surrendering to the police, Pop wrote a letter to Mom and confessed everything. It was Pop's turning point in his life. He exposed his lies, his real name, and the fact that he was turning himself in to begin a new chapter. Can you imagine receiving such a letter from someone you were dating?

The private man who had spent the last four-plus years hiding from FBI helicopters, evading wire tappings, surviving the Mexican cartel, and much more, was now coming clean and making himself known. Mom received Pop's letter through a mutual friend and wasn't sure if she would ever see the cowboy again.

On September 14, 1978, Pop and his pastor walked together into the San Diego police department. The scene did not go as expected. Pastor Torrell recalled seeing the cops pin Pop down and handcuff him on the spot. They led Pop away to be taken back to the east coast for trial. So much for the "more lenient" Southern California prisons.

Pop was eventually transferred back to Charleston, West Virginia where he stood in court to face his past. He was not alone. Pop's father, brother, sister, and even Pastor Torrell joined in support the day of the trial. After so many years, the moment was finally here. It was judgment day.

Ironically enough—or perhaps as a divine gift—the court could not find Pop's arrest warrant the day of his court trial. As this was the late 1970s, not everything had become digitized. They finally unearthed some of the dusty FBI notes on Pop, and the judge proceeded.

Pastor Torrell took the stand and portrayed the former drug dealer as a budding musician playing worship songs in church. Pop's father spoke how his son would have an opportunity to work in the family furniture business to be a contributing member to society. Then it was time for Pop to speak.

Pop shared how he was there to face his demons and past. He was not there to turn anyone else in or give names of those he worked with. He would accept whatever punishment the courts deemed necessary. Surprised at Pop's honesty and loyalty, the judge took a recess to consider what to do next. Everyone anxiously waited in the courthouse.

Eventually, they were all called back into the courtroom. The judge had made a decision. Pop would be convicted of the felony of drug-trafficking, but miraculously the judge waived all jail time.

Pop was restored to society and given another chance. By the end of 1979, Pop was back at the furniture store with his father, the same physical place he had been before the run, but a changed man in every other way.

After getting the verdict, Pop wrote Mom again.

This time he told her everything that had transpired. He invited her to visit Virginia, no longer living under an alias or out of a van with a couple of dogs like the first time they met.

Pop was hoping the cute blonde girl from California would also extend grace and provide him another opportunity to start again.

In a story that sounds more Hollywood than reality, Mom flew out to Virginia and fell back in love with the authentic version of Pop. They were married in 1982, and I was born shortly thereafter. I used to think that was always "supposed to happen." Now I consider my mere existence an absolute miracle!

Pop would later receive a full pardon of his felony conviction based on his changed life and community service record. He was restored back to full citizenship. On course to throw his life away, Pop did a 180-degree turn and took responsibility for his biggest mistakes in a way that hardly any man would. And he was not ashamed. It highlights the extent to which he worked on developing a life of personal integrity.

There are many more details, events, and miracles during his time on the run. The point is, he lived out an authentic life and learned how to become a provider the hard way. He stumbled out of the block as a prodigal son before forging the "Provider Wheel" habits.

As Pop shared this incredible story with me at the Lodge, I realized despite our baggage, we all can become providers by turning our story around.

CHAPTER SUMMARY

KEY TAKEAWAYS

- **We are called to go through suffering, not around it:** Avoidance is not a strategy that builds provider habits. We must face the challenge to get to the other side.
- **Our mistakes and insecurities make us authentic providers:** Life's experiences, especially our "learning moments," help us to develop the strength and compassion to provide for ourselves and others from a genuine desire.
- **Take responsibility, even if it's late in the game:** Doing the right thing will not be easy; but we can all leave a lasting provider legacy if we take steps today.

CHALLENGE

Identify an area in your life that you want to turn around. Confide in a trusted friend of your desire to move towards a new, intentional life that blesses and protects others.

---CHAPTER 11---

Always Provide

Why did Pop wait so long to share with us?

The better question might be, *Why did he decide to share his story at all?* Perhaps Pop was motivated to share his story so that we didn't hear it from someone else. He lamented that day during the story weekend at the Lodge, how he couldn't learn anything new about his father or grandparents who were all gone. This seemed to motivate him to share with us in person while he still could. He had no idea he only had days to live, or perhaps he sensed the end was near. I believe it was all God's timing.

The power of being known and sharing our story became real to me that day with Pop and my brother. I had never felt so close to my father. In fact, in the last journal entry before Pop passed away, I wrote:

> *"I spoke with Pop for the first time since last weekend's story, and it was a genuine, natural flowing conversation. What a gift."*

We never know how much longer we have to share our story. No one expected Pop's heart attack or even considered that his days were so limited. Having that weekend helped me quickly progress past the anger grieving stage after his death. How could I be angry? I was given a gift.

We can all overcome the desire to accept whatever happens to us by choosing to do the hard thing and start living intentionally. To begin providing for ourselves so we can serve others. Pop was faced with this harsh reality while on the run. He wanted to start a new life with Mom but couldn't while on the run. He first needed to take care of business.

We all need to take care of ourselves in order to do the same for others. Now you have some new tools at your disposal.

Armed with the Bless and Protect Matrix, the Provider Wheel, my experimentations, and the inspiration of Pop's transformation example, I hope you feel more equipped to start providing. But, get ready for unexpected challenges along the way.

A SECOND DEATH

We all know what it means to feel totally spent, only to be asked for more. To feel pain, only to endure a new injury before you have had time to fully heal.

Giving until it hurts forces you to either give up or to rely on God. We can burn out or we can lie down in green pastures, as Psalm 23 tells us, and receive the blessing and protection from our heavenly Shepherd to keep providing for others. I was tested between giving up or getting refueled when I received another terrible phone call.

"There has been a fire."

This time it was Mom on the line delivering the news. It had been just over three months since Pop's death, and now this. The Lodge was in flames.

After Pop's death, we had kept the Lodge largely untouched. Everything in it represented him and his lifestyle. From the mounted animal heads on the walls to his woodworking shop in the basement, it all embodied his passions and personality. Here was where Pop had breathed his final breath. Simply put, the house allowed us to feel connected with Pop in the wake of his loss.

And now it was forever changed.

I was stunned. I hurt for Mom again.

Mom had walked into the house to discover total devastation. Everything in the main living area had been charred and was completely black from the fire and subsequent smoke. There was a large hole burnt through the living room floor to the basement.

There were more questions than answers.

Sadly, we would learn that this was not a natural or accidental fire. It was an arson case.

Questions rattled our brains for the coming days, weeks, and months. Who did this? What on earth was the motivation? How could we move on from this?

We knew someone had broken into the Lodge, our private sanctuary. As if this first offense wasn't enough damage, the perpetrator(s) attempted to burn it all down. They poured gasoline and started a fire in the middle of the living room to destroy the house.

The local fire department and sheriff's office got involved. After arson was confirmed, the state police assigned an investigator. Our insurance company hired a senior fire investigator to review the case as well. This was serious.

No one had answers, but everyone agreed on one thing: this was a malicious arson attempt. The motivation was not theft, rather destroying the house. They left tools, firearms, even credit cards untouched. This frustrated the team of investigators and our family.

The investigators told us that if the perpetrator(s) had left a window open or door cracked in the house, it would have burned to the ground. Instead, the house was so tightly sealed that the fire lost oxygen and went out, but not before total devastation inside.

This hurt on many levels. I remember telling my wife that it felt like a second death. The house had been an unofficial memorial of Pop and his life; now, it was a hard place to return to, forever damaged. The house represented memories and stored precious items that allowed us to hold on to our previous reality as a family. Now that was taken away from us.

Instead of being allowed to grieve Pop's loss, we were thrust into an investigation and insurance claim that left us battered and torn emotionally as a family.

Going to the property and seeing it blocked off with yellow criminal tape deepened the feeling of loss.

After I got the call from Mom, I once again packed up the family and drove to see her, not knowing what to do. I wanted to be there for her but felt lost all the while—too familiar of a feeling.

This time, on top of grief, there was anger. There was frustration and hopelessness.

When I arrived at the Lodge, I paused before crossing the threshold which held so many memories.

This was where I felt closest to Pop. It was a sacred place, and it was now literally in ruins. The most significant physical reminder of Pop had been destroyed.

I had to hold my breath to protect myself from the fumes and gases of the smoldering house. I didn't want to face the destruction, but I knew I needed to. We had to take meticulous inventory of everything in the house, racking our brains to remember if anything was missing.

In our state of shock, we then had to answer scrutinizing questions from investigators trained to trip people up in their own words if this was an inside job just to collect an insurance claim. So while we were processing another loss, we were also being watched.

The arson expert kept asking the same questions and then it dawned on me—I was a suspect. Mom was a suspect. Our family was no longer protected at the Lodge; it was the focal point of a serious investigation.

I don't know what obstacles, difficult conversations, and hard places you are facing as you embark on your provider journey, but this is what I've learned: we need to return to the hard place in order to pass through tribulations. We are not called to avoid hardships, hoping for the best. Becoming a provider means we get to the other side by going through difficulties.

There was nothing else to do other than move forward with all parties and work toward rebuilding. It would serve as a physical representation of the rebuilding that needed to happen in our lives after the loss of Pop.

You may find, as I did, that you were truly given a gift in tragedy. Before Pop passed, I wasn't driven to provide. Now, even when I felt I had nothing to give, I knew I was providing by being willing to go through suffering rather than running away from it.

Unfortunately, the investigation fell short of any conclusive evidence, let alone convictions. We were left struggling to understand why this happened and how to rebuild. Sometimes the story doesn't end up as we hope, yet we are always called to provide through the uncertainties.

―――――

As we mentally build ourselves up to always provide, another critical question to ask is, who are we supposed to provide for in life?

Jesus provides us a guiding light through a story you are likely familiar with in Luke 10 with the story of Good Samaritan.

The story involves two "holy men" who pass by a beaten man who is in desperate need of help. The unexpected hero of the story is more of an outcast in society, but this Good Samaritan actually cares for the beaten man by taking him to the doctor and paying for all expenses.

Jesus summarizes the point of the story that we are all to be good neighbors and "go and do likewise" (English Standard Version).

I believe we miss the value of this parable if we debate and analyze which neighbor or individual to provide for; we are called to provide for those in need. So while the question, who should I provide for is reasonable, the better question is, are we "doing likewise"? Meaning, are we being the provider when we need to be?

How is it possible to provide for the needs all around us? I have felt overwhelmed at times, just trying to figure out my career and feeling like a failure time and time again. I get it.

Fortunately, Scripture provides wisdom in how we can discern a genuine need versus when our help is not needed. Remember, there are two equal components to providing: blessing and protecting. We are not expected to bless everyone all the time. Galatians 6:2-5 provides a beautiful and practical roadmap for knowing when you need to bless someone and when you need to protect them:

> Carry each other's burdens, and in this way, you will fulfill the law of Christ. If anyone thinks they are something when they are not, they deceive themselves. Each one should test their own actions. Then they can take pride in themselves alone, without comparing themselves to someone else, for each one should carry their own load.

This passage tells us that we are called to bless people when they have a burden, but we are also to protect people by not providing for small loads.

In the book *Boundaries,* Dr. Henry Cloud and Dr. John Townsend describe the difference between a burden and a daily load:

> The Greek words for burden and load give us insight into the meaning of these texts. The Greek word for burden means "excess burdens," or burdens that are so heavy that they weigh us down. These burdens are like boulders. They can crush us. We shouldn't be expected to carry a boulder by ourselves! It would break our backs. We need help with the boulders—those times of crisis and tragedy in our lives. (p. 32)

In contrast, the Greek word for load means "cargo" or "the burden of daily toil." This word describes the everyday things we all need to do. These loads are like knapsacks. Knapsacks are possible to carry. We are expected to carry our own. We are expected to deal with our own feelings, attitudes, and behaviors, as well as the responsibilities God has given to each one of us, even though it takes effort.

To become providers, we need to be wise in discerning when to bless others and when to protect them. This helps us from experiencing exhaustion and burnout. Galatians 6 provides an excellent resource in calling us to give ourselves sacrificially yet with wisdom and grace.

God's grace is never beyond our reach. As Pop's story shows, even when you are running away from your problems, you can be discovered.

As we conclude our journey together, let's not make Pop's story a trivial case study. His story represents a collective failure we all have of living a default life of passive living. When we don't make healthy decisions to invest in ourselves to bless others, we are passively going through this life hoping for the best even if we are actively running away!

Instead, I hope you take the information in the book and run with it.

I've provided an eight-week challenge in the appendix to help you stack each of the provider habits one at a time to introduce new healthy habits in your own life. It's more fun with an encouragement partner. There are also small groups through the CL Thomas Fellowship to offer additional support over a longer time commitment of nine months to help you dive deeper into the provider habits. The choice is yours. Just know that transformation is possible, and you get to decide right now what steps to take. With each decision, we are either moving with the comfort of passiveness, accepting whatever happens, or moving towards becoming an intentional provider with lifestyle changes.

Change is hard, and one group of researchers thought they knew why. Their hypothesis was people don't want to change until faced with life-and-death odds. So they tested this theory out by following patients who were suffering from a deadly heart disease. Physicians told these patients they had to adjust their lifestyle and diet. This was literally life-or-death stuff!

The researchers assumed 80% or more would make the change but only ~10% did. (Deutschman, 4)

That is a sobering and humbling statistic. It highlights how, although we may have been told all the facts to do something positive in our life, we may still not actually do them.

This research and statistics made a lasting impact on me since Pop passed away from a related coronary heart disease.

Fortunately the researchers kept digging into why the 10% changed and how eventually the doctors were able to get closer to that 80% mark. It wasn't through facts or fear, but through relationships. When patients were supported and encouraged through new connections to make hard changes, they were much more successful.

Don't let the desire to become a provider end here with only a thought. Take action. If you don't have a great support group currently, invest into building a healthier community around you so you can sustain the provider lifestyle.

If you are ready to take action, I invite you to start an eight-week provider habit-building challenge that I call the Matter Ladder. Each week you practice one of the provider habits until you have added one new habit per week into your schedule. Please see Appendix I at the end of this book for the details.

I'm committed to this work and to support your provider journey.

Bless and Protect!
Justin Thomas

————————NEXT STEPS————————

CHALLENGE

If you are looking for a place to start, I've created an eight-week challenge called the Matter Ladder in the appendix of this book. It proposes weekly habits to try to master, one provider habit a week. I hope it serves as a practical next step on your journey!

Access my latest resources on my website at justinthomascoaching.com, and for more information on the CL Thomas Fellowship with groups for men and women, go to clthomasfellowship.org.

I was once again wearing Pop's leather vest.

Similar to Pop's funeral reception, I looked out into a room filled with friends, family, and mentors. Except for tonight, we were not just celebrating Pop's life but his provider legacy. Tonight's event was a celebration dinner commemorating the successful launch and completion of the first CL Thomas Fellowship class.

Sometimes you need to throw a party in life. I wanted to celebrate the wins of life in the face of its harsh new realities. This dinner event turned out to be one of the most memorable evenings of my life.

We had family members drive in from out of state to attend. We even had friends from abroad fly in for the dinner event. The men who just completed the fellowship were in attendance along with their wives. Several of my mentors were present. It was a room full of people who had poured into my life and also into the fellowship. Most importantly, Mom was there.

We enjoyed dinner together and then I stood up. It was time to share how the year went and the tools we use to help us become providers.

I showed a testimonial video highlighting the first fellowship class and how their definition of "provider" had expanded. I then shared how we were scaling the fellowship beyond me and equipping other men to lead their own groups. It was exciting news. Then I announced this book project for the first time publicly. I read excerpts about Pop and how he provided and my struggle to understand how to provide like Pop. When I finished sharing all of these exciting updates, I felt the night had been a grand success. However, the most powerful moment was still coming.

As people started to leave, they thanked me for a great evening and congratulated me on the fellowship. It had been a special moment and I was starting to feel pretty good about all the planning I had done. Yet the night was not about me and my effort. Fortunately, God showed this to me by directing my attention to Mom's table. I looked over from the front of the room where I was collecting my items from the podium and witnessed the men who had just completed the fellowship program get up in unison and walk over to Mom's table.

The guys introduced themselves one by one to Mom in a respectful, honoring fashion. I was immediately struck with the scene unfolding before my eyes as I witnessed these men become providers.

I proudly looked on as I saw one fellowship graduate after another hug Mom as she cried into their arms tears of joy, pain, and gratitude all wrapped into one. They had blessed and protected her. This moment represented all of the provider characteristics. This not only made my night but also Mom's and she sent me this message afterwards to honor the moment:

> One of the most meaningful, special nights of my life. I will always enjoy the memory. It's just so incredible to see your vision alive and in a way that is so honoring to Pop. He was a very unique man, and it is very rewarding to see his life have an impact on young men. What a great group of people gathered together tonight!

I continue to find new ways of pushing myself in order to support others better. Running has become a new hobby and I willed myself to complete my first marathon in honor of Pop. This "race" turned out to be a solo virtual contest in March of 2020 because as you remember, the world shut down. However, our world still needs us to continue to grow and improve because the challenges are ever-increasing.

The podcast "Become a Provider" was birthed during the pandemic and guess what—I got the legendary Bob Goff to join as a guest! One of my absolute favorite episodes is #5, where my brother and I reflect on some of the bonus stories that did not make it in this book about Pop and his time on the run.

I continue to learn from my colleagues at dooable health and we are proving it is possible to have fun while working on big, hairy, audacious goals together.

I promised my family this would be my last revision and I'd work on a new book, so be on the lookout for more in the future! Until then, I encourage us all to become better providers; it's who we are called to be. We are all gifted in a unique way to bless and protect one another. A provider invests in themselves in order to give sacrificially. It will hurt and stretch you beyond what you think is possible. Then you will experience the blessing and promise that Psalm 23 provides: "The Lord is my shepherd, I shall not want." You will be provided for over and over again so that you can do the same to those in your spheres of influence.

I'm committed to this work for life. I have no idea how small or large God wants this provider movement to go and what role this book, the podcast, my speaking or the CL Thomas Fellowship will have, but I know it will be a grand adventure.

I consider myself lucky and blessed to have had Pop as a father who allowed me to know my heavenly Father, Jesus.

Enjoy blessing and protecting others.

ACKNOWLEDGMENTS

Pop's unexpected death introduced the most significant test of how my family lives with joy. I can honestly say this was both the hardest and the most rewarding period of my life. Re-writing this update forced me to clarify the lessons I learned and reminded me of all the people who breathed life into this project when I needed inspiration to complete.

Mom, this book is dedicated to you for a reason. Thank you for your prayers; they have been powerful and effective in my life and I continue to be blessed by you. I hope that this book provided for you in a small way.

To my lovely lady, my wife, Amy. I have benefited from your strength when I was at my weakest. You allowed me space to grieve and the freedom to dream. You also get all the bonus points and gold stars for hearing my barrage of ideas and editing an unimaginable number of my manuscripts. Thank you for not only making this book better based on your direct feedback, but for making me a better man. Thank you for choosing me.

To my brother, John. A man whom I respect and with whom I can be fully known. Thank you for your support and encouragement. Pop would be so proud of how you serve your family selflessly.

Writing a book about the story of losing your father is a challenging process. I'm forever indebted to my sister-in-law and editor, Sophie, who guided me from start to finish with professionalism and empathy.

To Sister Amie. My love is unconditional. Pop would have loved seeing how you have stepped up to support Mom.

To the extended Thomas Family. You held our family up when we needed a lift. From prayers we heard in person to all the silent ones I know you whispered in your own quiet times with the Lord. You have served as God's hands and feet for our family in practical ways since Pop's passing. Thank you dearly.

To the men and women who have been part of a CL Thomas Fellowship. Thank you for investing into yourselves and honoring the legacy of Pop in your own unique way.

To my colleagues at dooable health who demonstrate health and wellness each and every day. You inspire and remind me how to invest in myself while serving others. It's a privilege to learn from you Dr. Joe, Dr. B.J., Jeanine, and Sarah.

To Bob Goff, the encourager to millions and me! I am living with more whimsy and dreaming big thanks to you.

To Tim Oakley and our men's group. God placed you all in my life to prepare a solid foundation for the challenges I endured after our group ended. I respect and love you.

To the men of Dayspring Park. Over the past twenty-five years we have literally grown up together through middle school, playing basketball, and now as we continue to compete in our fantasy football league. I hope I beat you all. Thank you for your support.

To Coach Dug Hampton, my unofficial book PR rep:) Your support means the world to me. From teaching me the fundamentals of basketball to the game of life, you have been a constant and positive voice in my life. Thank you.

To Pop's friends. Thank you for sharing stories of his life escapades. I know you would not want to be named publicly—especially for harboring a fugitive! You demonstrated loyalty and love through thick and thin.

To the men of F3 Churham who push me every week to improve

my fitness, fellowship, and faith. Thank you for strengthening and challenging me.

To Pastor Reggie and Bomi. Your friendship, mentorship, and support has been a blessing for over a decade. Thank you for serving as advisors from the beginning of our nonprofit work together.

To my coaching clients, thank you for trusting me and putting in the hard work of making real change. It is a privilege to see your transformations.

To all the people who support the CL Thomas Fellowship; from the men who trust me to guide them along their personal provider journey to my mentors who pour into the program. Reaching between North Carolina and Ireland, you are all making a real difference!

Finally, to my daughters, Penny and Edie. Thank you for your motivation to become a better provider and for all the "help" when I was writing by sitting on my lap, drawing next to me, and for the fun trampoline breaks in between writing sessions.

Thank you all.

Please share how your provider journey is going by emailing me at justin@justinthomascoaching.com.

WORKS CITED

Brown, Brene. *Gifts of Imperfection.* Hazelden, 2010.

Chambers, Oswald. *My Utmost for His Highest.*
Barbour Publishing, 1963.

Cloud, Dr. Henry, and Dr. John Townsend. *Boundaries.*
HarperCollins, 2017.

DEA. "Drug Enforcement Agency." *The Early Years,*
2019, https://www.dea.gov/sites/default/files/2018-
07/Early%20Years%20p%2012-29%20%281%
29.pdf. Accessed 15 July 2019.

Deutschman, Alan. *Change or Die.* HarperCollins,
2007.

English Standard Version. The Holy Bible. *Crossway
Bibles, 2016.*

Goggins, David. *Can't Hurt Me.* Lioncrest, 2018.

GoRuck. "GoRuck Tribe." *Seek Pain in 2021*, 2021, https://www.goruck.com/pages/tribe. Accessed 2 September 2021.

Huberman, Andrew. "The Tim Ferriss Show." *Dr. Andrew Huberman — A Neurobiologist on Optimizing Sleep, Performance, and Testosterone (#521)*, 2021, https://tim.blog/2021/07/08/andrew-huberman-transcript/. Accessed 7th November 2021.

Lewis, C.S. *The Four Loves.* HarperOne, 2017.

McRaven, William. "Make Your Bed Speech." *University of Texas at Austin as Commencement Speech*, 2014, https://www.youtube.com/watch?v=LoKdCqgiSVY. Accessed 7 November 2021.

Merriam-Webster. "Provide." *Definition of provide*, 2021, https://www.merriam-webster.com/dictionary/provide. Accessed 2 September 2021.

Miller, James E. *Winter Grief, Summer Grace: Returning to Life After a Loved One Dies.* Fortress Press, 1995.

New King James Version. *The Bible.* Thomas Nelson, 1982.

New Living Translation. *The Bible.* Tyndale House, 2015.

Peterson, Jordan B. *12 Rules for Life: An Antidote to Chaos.* Random House Canada, 2018.

Pfeiffer, Charles. *The Wycliffe Bible Commentary.* R.R.
Donnelley & Sons Company, 1968.

Matter Ladder Challenge

Climb the Matter Ladder: In eight weeks, you will develop habits that will make you a provider and leader who matters. It's a practical and strategic way of investing into yourself and others.

Why is it called the Matter Ladder? We do this to be leaders who matter. Each day that we complete our daily challenges, we climb up the ladder towards our goal of becoming the person we wish to be.

What is this? It's an eight-week challenge that you can do solo or, better yet, with one or two other friends to increase accountability. The goal is to create healthy new habits to make yourself better for others and experience a personal breakthrough.

What are the requirements? Daily completion of the assigned tasks for eight weeks. See the next page for a review of the specific challenges over the eight-week period. It's going to be great!

To learn more about the Matter Ladder Challenge, visit
justinthomascoaching.com/matterladder.

MATTER LADDER WEEKLY SCHEDULE

Each week you add a new challenge on top of what you were doing the week before. By the end of the eight-week challenge, you have introduced all the habits in the Provider Wheel. If you mess up, practice personal integrity by acknowledging the setback to yourself and perhaps a "provider partner" and keep going!

	Week 1	Week 2	Week 3	Week 4	Week 5	Week 6	Week 7	Week 8
Blessing Speaker: Write a daily note of encouragement to someone.	X	X	X	X	X	X	X	X
Personal Integrity: Finish at least 1 commitment you made.		X	X	X	X	X	X	X
Be There: Schedule at least 1 activity with someone you love, doing what they love to do.			X	X	X	X	X	X
Prepared: Do one thing each day that will make tomorrow better or easier.				X	X	X	X	X
Biblical Generosity: Joyfully sacrifice 1 hour this week for someone else.					X	X	X	X
Prayerful: Pray/meditate for 5 consecutive minutes per day.						X	X	X
Be Known: Share something to a trusted friend/family member that you have never shared.							X	X
Physically Fit: Try going a week without drinking any sugar (bonus points for limiting sugar from your overall diet as well) *disclaimer if you are on medication for regulating blood sugar please consult your healthcare provider*								X

ABOUT THE AUTHOR

Justin Thomas is a National Board-Certified Health and Wellness Coach, successful entrepreneur, and average fantasy football player. He is the co-founder of The C.L. Thomas Fellowship, a nonprofit mentoring organization with groups currently meeting in America and Ireland. Justin also is a principal at dooable health, podcast host, and a personal coach to business leaders. Justin's greatest ambitions in life are to hear the words "well done, good and faithful servant;" dreaming big with his family; having fun; and building enduring companies.

Justin's work has been featured in Forbes, Fox, Faith Driven Entrepreneur, and JAMA Internal Medicine. He also offers insights into how to live a sustainable life on his podcast, "Become a Provider." He lives in Hillsborough, NC with his wife and two daughters. You may see him running around town or on the trails as he trains for his next endurance event.

See all of Justin's work at www.justinthomascoaching.com.

CPSIA information can be obtained
at www.ICGtesting.com
Printed in the USA
BVHW031749080322
630921BV00001B/75

9 780578 334141